TRAUMATIC STRESS RECOVERY

David A. Fohrman, M.D.

First published by Dog Ear Publishing
4010 W. 86th Street, Ste H
Indianapolis, IN 46268
www.dogearpublishing.net

dog ear
PUBLISHING

ISBN: 978-1-4575-1778-5

This book is printed on acid-free paper.

Printed in the United States of America

TABLE OF CONTENTS

Part II: The GROWTH Model – Competency-Based Recovery

Part III: Additional Actions to Help Veterans

Introduction

Talk about Post-Traumatic Stress Disorder (PTSD) and war has become so pervasive that we can hardly turn anywhere—newspapers, magazines, television programs, and indeed books—without confronting some new headline about the disorder's harsh effects on hundreds of thousands of afflicted veterans. In many ways this attention is long overdue and much deserved; veterans of foreign wars are not only susceptible to trauma in combat, but also likely to encounter non-combat related traumatic events as well. Symptoms of post-traumatic stress are an extremely common result, and it's not a problem from which we can afford to turn away. And it's not only veterans who suffer: police officers, rescue workers, EMTs, and others whose jobs demand they continue to function competently even in catastrophic, profoundly disturbing, life threatening situations are also at risk. The reality of post-traumatic stress thus extends over an enormous swath of modern society. The focus of this book is to help traumatized deployed veterans. However, the same ideas and techniques can help veterans of any profession who routinely risk their lives to help or protect others.

Myths and misconceptions about PTSD—that the condition is permanent and incurable, or that it only affects "weak-minded" individuals—cause many traumatized veterans to suffer in silence and shame. Many consider or attempt suicide to bring finality to their suffering. Throughout this book, I strive to bring out truths about post-traumatic stress that will help veterans and others understand how trauma affects everything from the creation of memories to the destruction of basic beliefs. We'll look at ways to "fix" traumatic memories and to rebuild these basic beliefs, as well as introduce a systematic, evidence-based, six-step method of natural recovery from trauma. Trauma is often said to be inescapable, and in some sense this is true, just as with every other experience from a person's past. But as traumatized veterans build their ability to undo the biological and psychological causes of post trauma stress in constructive, healthy ways, they progress along a path of recovery toward fulfilling, interconnected lives.

Developing this ability isn't a matter for the intellect. Recovery is, in fact, based on *experiences* and depends on developing very specific *skills*. After a series of sacrifices on the field of battle, veterans need to re-learn how to have a range of experiences that are not only common, but are largely taken for granted in any civilian's daily life. These experiences include feeling safe, trusting others, and being able to give and accept help. To make this shift, veterans need support from people they know and respect. Some of this support comes from medical doctors, government facilitators, psychiatrists and therapists. More and more, the support veterans need comes from their friends, families, co-workers, and members of their community. I call these people veteran "helpers", and they play an essential role in easing a veteran's deployment-related psychological suffering.

As a matter of survival, soldiers train, pack and prepare for every mission. They can't afford to overthink a situation once the bombs start dropping and the bullets begin to fly. Ideally, soldiers, airmen, sailors, and marines are given the training—prior to deployment—they need to face, endure and recover from the long-term psychiatric effects of combat. The truth, however, is that there is no exhaustive, all-encompassing method of preparing the mind for the effects of trauma. Upon a veteran's return from war, he or she must continue to learn how to recover if post-traumatic stress symptoms don't resolve on their own. This book provides veterans, leaders, and veteran helpers with a roadmap to guide their progress to a new environment of strength, safety, compassion and trust. The explanations and methods are as direct and concise as possible. Definitions are kept succinct, and elaboration to a minimum.

In the long run, traumatized veterans often achieve a higher level of function than they would have if the trauma had not occurred. For military personnel, this means a more efficient fighting force; one that is not "damaged" or "broken" as a result of trauma, but rather even more capable, and motivated, to do whatever is necessary to successfully accomplish their mission. This would represent a dramatic shift from the current status quo where all veterans with a diagnosis of PTSD are delegated to get the same treatment; independent of the symptom severity or the existence of co-occurring strengths or weaknesses. The result is that the average veteran suffers in silence for approximately five years prior to asking for help - in a system that labels them with a permanent, most likely incurable, problem - and offers financial reward based on the degree to which veterans remain "sick" and functionally impaired.

The knowledge and approach presented in this book is based on years of classes, sessions, seminars and research I've conducted with traumatized veterans, some of whom were referred to me only after decades of treatment for PTSD with little success. I've seen these methods work first-hand to improve the lives of thousands of veterans and their loved ones. Their symptoms of post-traumatic stress did not magically disappear - rather, with time, effort, and work - these veterans gained hope where previously there was none, in their ability to conquer and ultimately control, intolerable, unending suffering.

The book is divided into three parts. **Part I** gives the reader essential information about the biological and psychological causes of PTSD, as well as the connection between deployment-related trauma and subsequent thoughts of suicide. **Part II** presents a six-step, competency-based program veterans can use to dramatically decrease the impact of chronic PTSD-type problems. **Part III** addresses the question of what we, as a community, can do to help veterans and others at risk for developing PTSD. This involves actively challenging assumptions about what it means to be "healthy," "productive," "strong," "capable" and "cured." In addition, I show how families, community members and leaders can use functional indicators to help encourage suffering veterans to get the help they need. The three sections of this book build on each other when read in sequence, but they can also be helpful when read as "stand-alone" subsections.

Case examples and clinical vignettes are kept to a minimum. This book assumes the reader has a familiarity with the type of traumatic experiences service members can face while deployed as well as the type of long-term problems they can experience after getting out of the military. For those interested in learning more about how post-traumatic stress can present itself in Combat Veterans please see Appendix A for additional resources. Lastly, for the sake of brevity, the book provides only an overview of the types of practical exercises one can use to help veterans decrease the intensity and severity of PTSD-type symptoms. Please refer to the companion book, *The Traumatic Stress Recovery for Veterans: Workbook* available through www.resiliencyservices.com, for additional practical exercises.

Part I

Combat, PTSD, and Thoughts of Self Harm – A Lethal Triad

CHAPTER ONE

What is PTSD?

If you or a loved one has served in the military, especially over the last decade, you've most likely heard of Post-Traumatic Stress Disorder, or PTSD. Over the past several years, even everyday Americans have absorbed the widespread media coverage of the causes, effects, treatments and stories of veterans with PTSD. Whether you understand PTSD at the level of psychological analysis or popular culture, the fundamentals are the same: PTSD is a dangerous, debilitating condition that can negatively impact the lives of veterans and their families for years, or even decades, after they've been discharged.

The DSM-IV-TR, the American Psychiatric Association's seminal work on mental disorders, defines PTSD according to a specific set of criteria common to all people who suffer from this disorder. These criteria arise from, and can continue long after, traumatic events, including, but not limited to, experiences in war. The criteria, divided into groups A, B, C and D describe a range of experiences and symptoms that can help veterans and veteran helpers understand the nature of the condition. Here's a short primer on what these symptoms are and why an understanding of them is so important to recovering from PTSD.

Symptom Criterion A: Exposure to Trauma

When we think of "trauma," we think of shock, sudden or violent loss, upheaval, and devastation. Trauma is more than hurt or unpleasantness, more than mere "trouble." Trauma causes people to fear for their lives, question core beliefs about the world, or feel utterly helpless. By definition, traumatic events are unexpected, chaotic experiences beyond a person's anticipation or control. As one Vietnam vet put it, ambushing the enemy was not traumatic. Getting ambushed was.

Countless news reports talk about the difficulties faced by veterans returning home from combat, but combat is not the only reason that veterans develop PTSD. Military Sexual Trauma, or MST, is a tragically common occurrence for both men and women serving in the armed forces. And service members are as prone as civilians to traumatic events, such as the unexpected death of a loved one or a serious auto accident.

Concerning the nature of traumatic events, one thing is essential to keep in mind: Trauma is not defined solely in terms of the scale of destruction or horror. What makes an event traumatic is not how disgusting, horrendous, or gory it may (or may not) seem to an outside observer. Rather, all instances of trauma are linked to an event that is perceived as profoundly *unfair.* Hence, killing an enemy combatant who was trying to kill you does not qualify, from the perspective of biology and psychology, as a traumatic event, because the act was committed in all fairness for the preservation of self and others. Accidently killing a child, however, defies all definition of something "fair."

The terrorist attacks of September 11, 2001 were traumatic for most Americans not only because they snuffed out the lives of thousands, but because the terrorists' acts were unthinkable, unimaginable, and against the "rules." Before 9/11, we went about our daily lives without worrying that someone would launch a hijacked passenger plane into a skyscraper like a guided missile. Such an outrageous action goes against the basic rules we assume are shared by everyone else in the modern world. The 9/11 attacks caused trauma because they jolted those basic assumptions out from under our feet. The potentially traumatic events veterans witness or experience during wartime can be large or small in scale, sometimes affecting thousands of human beings, sometimes affecting just one. But the realization that an event was horribly unfair or against the rules is a large part of what renders it traumatic.

The final element is care or compassion for the person or persons involved in the event. This can change over time. Some veterans may only feel concern or have been bothered if either they themselves or a close friend were severely wounded or killed. Others, especially those in a position of authority, may be affected by the deaths of subordinates for whom they were responsible. Still others can feel intense empathy and be traumatized by the deaths of civilians, or even specific enemy combatants. In every case, however, veterans are only traumatized if the persons involved were dear to them.

Symptom Criterion B: Reliving the Event

One of the most insidious things about PTSD is that memories of a traumatic event can resurface at any time. Worse, the unexpected emergence of traumatic memories can often create a feeling even more intense than the traumatic event itself. Veterans can experience overwhelming terrors during the day and horrifying dreams at night. Even though the event is over, these symptoms make it feel present and inescapable.

The feeling that you're actually reliving a traumatic event is called a flashback. Flashbacks have triggers: sounds, sights, or smells that causes a person to experience a past traumatic event as if it were happening right now. Some triggers are obvious, like fireworks on the Fourth of July reminding a veteran of live fire on the battlefield. Other triggers aren't obvious at all. Veterans may not know that some seemingly innocuous sight, sound, smell, or body position causes them to recall a trauma from the past. When this happens, veterans are doubly disturbed. First, they have to deal with the immediate effect of this "intrusive recollection." Second, they have to deal with the fact that they don't know how, when or why it may all happen again.

Symptom Criterion C: Avoidance and Numbing

Once they begin to recognize the triggers for flashbacks or intrusive memories, veterans do everything they can to avoid them. This includes avoiding situations and people they previously enjoyed or loved. It also means that veterans may cease to talk or even think about the traumatic event, or anything or anyone associated with it. Imagine you had been in a head-on collision. Months have passed and your physical wounds have healed. But any time you talk about getting behind the wheel, you feel as if you're being smashed, shaken, and belted all over again. Veterans often avoid talking about their trauma, because doing so brings that trauma back to life.

Avoidance is accompanied by pressure to numb the emotional effects of traumatic events. Veterans with PTSD often find it very difficult to feel, let alone express emotions, whether those emotions are good or bad. Veterans who used to be outgoing and affectionate may become closed off and "hard to read." As a result, many veterans have serious problems with long-term relationships. Many get divorced or separated. Among those who stay married, the spouse often feels as if the veteran is keeping them at an emotional arm's length. There's a coldness to personal interactions, resulting from an inability to emotionally communicate.

For these reasons, which constitute the destruction of basic beliefs, veterans with PTSD often lose interest in activities they used to love. They lack the passion that drove them to tackle new challenges, or keep up with those activities they used to enjoy. Finally, PTSD-afflicted veterans often have a sense of a "foreshortened future," that their lives will not be as meaningful or even as long as those of others. They feel they're likely to die young, never form a meaningful relationship, never be successful or make any positive impact on the world.

Symptom Criterion D: Hyperarousal

Younger veterans, in particular, are what we call "wired for sound." They can be jittery, always on the alert, and obsessively attuned to signs of danger. You can tell a veteran is hyperaroused—or “keyed up”—when they sit with their back against the wall of a restaurant or other public setting, keeping their environment (and any perceived threats therein) in full view. They frequently look over their shoulders to check their flanks or “six.”[1] Other signs of hyperarousal include unprovoked or sudden shows of anger or irritability, as well as insomnia and the inability to concentrate.

SYMPTOM CRITERION E: TIME

An official diagnosis of PTSD comes only after an individual has experienced symptoms for more than one month.[2] In actual practice, especially in cases of repeated or prolonged exposure to trauma—for example, those that can occur when a veteran is deployed—clinicians often wait at least six months to make a PTSD diagnosis. It is also important to differentiate between *symptoms* of post-traumatic stress, which are often self-limiting and not a sign of long-term impairment, and a formal diagnosis of PTSD; loved ones and other untrained individuals can identify and help to assuage symptoms, while an official diagnosis of PTSD should only be made by a qualified mental health professional.[3]

Not every veteran will have every one of the symptoms described above, and some veterans will experience unique symptoms beyond those we’ve touched on here. But by keeping these signs and symptoms in mind, you’ve taken a powerful first step toward understanding where veterans are coming from as they grapple with the effects of post-traumatic stress.

CHAPTER 2

PTSD is not a "Logical" Problem

Solving problems logically is something we do so often it's second nature. Fiction's famous detective Sherlock Holmes called it the "science of deduction." We have before us certain facts about a problem. To find a solution, we use these facts to come to a logical conclusion. Problem solved, we move on.

Here's an example of solving a relatively simple, everyday problem with deductive reasoning: A friend calls and says to meet him at the movie theater to see a new release at 6:00 p.m., but he doesn't specify which theater. How can you figure out where he will be at six? You have a number of facts you can use to deduce the answer logically: two of your town's five theaters are discount venues and only show older movies; since your friend wanted to see a new release, they're off the table. Of the remaining three, only two are showing the movie your friend wants to see. Of these two, only one is within walking distance of your friend's house, and he doesn't own a car. Problem solved—you know where to show at 6:00 p.m. and can logically expect your friend to be there.

But what if we're missing a key piece of information, something that, if we knew it, would change our entire way of thinking about the problem? What if, for example, your friend failed to mention that his sister was coming, too, and would drive him to the theater across town? All the logic in the world wouldn't have told you this, and without this knowledge, you are bound to show up at the wrong place.

Ideally, of course, we have all the information necessary to come to a logical conclusion. Hence, in a perfect world your friend (to keep with our example above) would have told you the specific name and location of the place he wanted to meet. In cases like this, which characterize most of the problems we face in everyday life, logic prevails. The baby needs diapers. The grocery store up the street is open and sells diapers. Hence, I'll head to the grocery store up the street. We have little to deduce, little to guess at, and we can therefore make confident decisions that result in sure, expected, logical outcomes. But PTSD is different, because sufferers don't have key, essential information they need to "solve" their problem. Without this information, logic malfunctions, leaving veterans to guess at a solution. Too often they guess wrong, and things get worse.

PTSD and the Brain

We tend to think of the brain as the seat of brilliance, or at least of ideas. The brain thinks, it dreams, it produces endorphins and sparks neurons that fill us with feelings of love, hate, happiness, and remorse. Most importantly, the brain solves logical problems. But PTSD fundamentally impairs a person's ability to problem-solve, think, and feel. Here are some facts about the inner workings of the brain that every veteran and veteran helper needs to know.

The human brain is made up of many different layers or parts, some very advanced (that is, the parts that make us human), and others less sophisticated (that is, the parts of the brain that are similar to a dog's, a rat's, or even a lizard's brain). If you took your brain and shaved off the top few millimeters, you'd be left with the brain of an ape. Shave off some more and you'd have the brain of the average dog or cat. The innermost core of the human brain—the part known as the "limbic brain"—is essentially the same as a lizard's. What elevates our brains above those of lizards and other animals lies in our brains' uppermost layer.

When veterans get PTSD, the limbic brain intermittently highjacks the human part of the brain. To picture this, make a fist with the top of your thumb tucked inside. Now turn your hand so that your thumb faces you. This is a rough picture of what your brain would be like if split down the middle. Your thumb represents the limbic brain, with your index finger as the human brain that wraps around it. FIGURE BELOW

Representation of the locations of the top, "human" brain and the middle, more primitive, "limbic" brain.

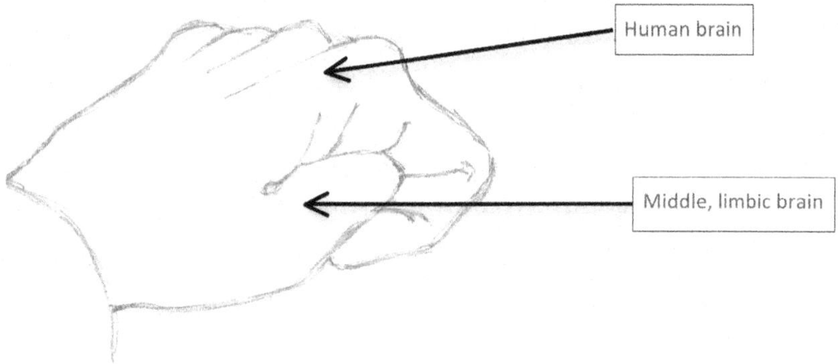

These parts of the brain are physically separate from each other; the human brain sends commands to the limbic brain, which, under normal circumstances, it follows. The limbic brain can also act independently to stimuli by using "primitive logic," not the "human logic" we use consciously every day. Since trauma directly affects the limbic brain, we need to find ways other than logic and deductive reasoning to motivate and condition its behavior—that is, so that we can stimulate the brain to do things that will help veterans get better.

How to Motivate the Limbic Brain to Solve Problems

The key point is this: The top, human brain learns and solves problems using logic; the inner, limbic brain learns, records, and "thinks" by using association.

You can't motivate or change the limbic brain with the force of logic or reason. These "languages," if you will, are not understood. Here it's helpful to think about the classic experiment of a rat in a maze. When you want to get the rat to move in a particular direction, no amount of reasoning with it will work. Ask the rat to do it, do it right, or do it faster, and he'll simply twitch his whiskers. What he needs is encouragement in the form of positive or negative re-enforcement[4]. Want the rat to go straight? Reward him with a piece of cheese when he moves forward. Want to discourage the rat from going forward? Give him a mild electric shock. What happens if you sequentially give a rat a positive reward (cheese) and then, when he tries to get it, an adverse one (a mild shock)? The rat will react—that is, go for the cheese or not—based on whichever stimulus, positive or negative, is greater.

Rats' Reactions and Learned Behaviors Based on Sum of Positive and Negative Responses

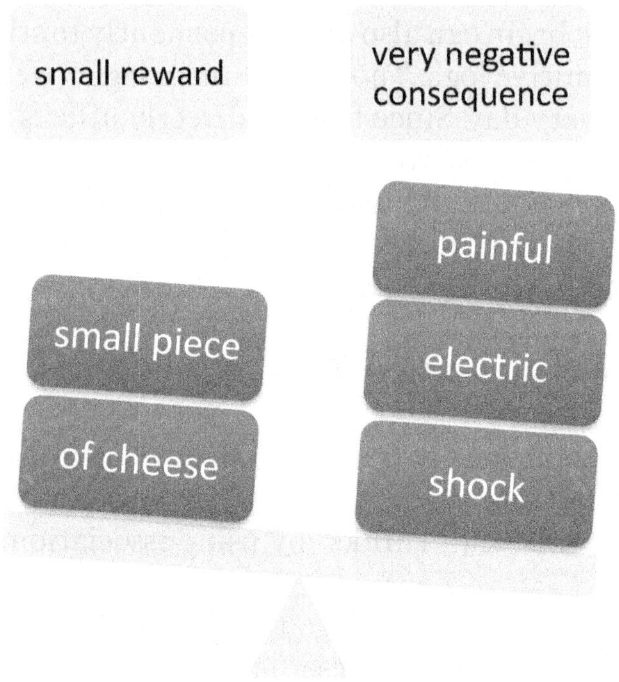

In this example, the adverse response is greater than the reward, so after a few trials, a hungry rat will not try to get the cheese, *even if it's obvious that the rat will not receive a shock for the attempt (because the device that emits the electric shock has been removed).*

Veterans with PTSD inadvertently follow a similar learning process. The logic of the human brain may tell them one thing, but their limbic brain, which is based on experience, drives them on. Traumatized veterans who feel extremely anxious, angry, or upset will often think about healthy ways to decrease their extreme negative feelings: countering them by thinking positive thoughts, for example, or calming them through practices such as deep, measured breathing. This is, in fact, a sound approach; the problem is that these techniques don't match the intensity of the negative feelings—thoughts of a pleasant summer day with friends are overwhelmed by feelings of hatred and horror associated with a traumatic experience in combat; attempts to breath calmly and collectedly are overwhelmed by hyperventilation or hyperarousal during a panic attack or flashback. Consequently, veterans "learn" that these healthy, potentially life-saving techniques *DO NOT WORK*. And they would be right—if PTSD-related competencies were rooted in logic. But in fact they are rooted in *skills*. The solution to recovering from PTSD-type symptoms requires this shift in paradigms, and it's neither intuitive nor obvious.

For veterans trying to come to terms with the effects of trauma, the situation is analogous to one where a novice skier begins at the top of an extremely steep, expert-level slope. The descent is going to be rough—assuming the skier makes it down alive, and moreover that he or she really wants to continue to learn to ski, they face a dilemma: keep on at this rate and risk serious injury or death, or give up on trying to learn to ski. Trauma-afflicted veterans face a similar dilemma when it comes to tackling the symptoms of trauma, with an additional unexpected complication.

The Orienting Response and PTSD

Our limbic brain is hardwired to react almost instantly (in about 12 milliseconds) to a perceived danger. Next (in about 30 milliseconds) comes the reaction of the human brain in the form of an "orienting response"—you stop, look around, and identify the perceived threat in your environment. Finally, you take appropriate action; if the threat's a snarling lion, you run or attack; if it's just a housecat that knocked over some dishes, you take a big sigh and calm down. With PTSD-related problems, the orienting response doesn't work, because the cause of the response was a benign stimulus—not a threatening, dangerous one. A benign stimulus could be something like a color or scent that happened to be present at the time of the trauma. The human brain can't identify the cause of the orienting response, and this accelerates and amplifies emotion—if a veteran was scared, he gets more scared; if angry, more angry. It's especially important to understand that positive emotions, such as those associated with intimacy, can be triggers. This can cause serious problems for veterans' relationships with others.

The net result is veterans with PTSD are not only unable to fix PTSD-type problems, they can't even identify the context or situations when these symptoms will occur. They trust that their brains will accurately identify and make them aware of potential dangers so that they can adjust, adapt, and steer clear—just as the novice skier trusts that his skis won't break or malfunction on the way down the treacherous slope.

Sometimes, unpredictably, a veteran's anxiety shoots to "panic level": shortness of breath, tensing muscles, racing pulse. Veterans don't want to dwell on their anxiety all the time, so they pick their battles, putting off lesser feelings of anxiety as they go about their daily lives, but facing panic-level anxiety head on. This means veterans are likely to try to stop feelings of anxiety when those feelings are raging and most likely to overwhelm any attempts to shut them down. Using techniques like measured breathing and meditation as part of an orienting response to calm oneself down is important—it's a logical, rational response to anxiety—but these techniques aren't effective in a state of panic. Veterans need to train the limbic brain to respond to anxiety while their anxious feelings are least intense—much like the rat in the maze, they need to associate positive feelings with safe people, places, and things, and associate negative feelings with situations of real or potential danger. By doing so, veterans are developing the skills—not just the rationale—for dealing with anxiety and other problems associated with PTSD.

So what does this mean for veterans with PTSD-type symptoms? The short answer is that PTSD is largely characterized by fears, anxiety, anger, and other intense emotions that won't go away simply because someone tries to convince him or herself that these feelings don't make sense. A veteran needs, instead, to learn specific, competency-based skills that will help dramatically decrease the intensity of these emotions.

CHAPTER 3

The Biologic Origins of PTSD

PTSD is the Result of a Vicious Cycle

PTSD is a biological phenomenon that results from a vicious cycle in the brain. The limbic brain keeps activating partially processed, trauma-induced memories while the "human" brain scrambles to make these extremely unpleasant recollections go away. Of course, they don't go away, but retreat back into the limbic brain where they struggle again to be exposed. The cycle keeps repeating, and PTSD takes root in the psychological criteria A through D that we outlined in Chapter 1. Here's a quick review of how the process works.

You're exposed to a potentially life-threatening event, and experience subsequent feelings of horror and helplessness. Soldiers witness scenes of horror that they could not have imagined. When this happens, the brain responds by creating a trauma-induced, abnormal memory of that event.

You can re-experience the traumatic event through memory. Unlike normal, long-term, autobiographical memories

(memories of your first bike ride, for example), which you can recall as pleasure, traumatic memories are thrust into consciousness seemingly at random—not because we want to think about them again. The return of trauma-induced memories happens without our control, but rather through sensory triggers that trip an emotional switch and bring the trauma back to light.

You experience feelings of numbing and avoidance, attempts to suppress the hurt caused by memories of trauma. When veterans experience flashbacks and other intrusive recollections of a prior trauma, they may think they're losing their minds. Hence, they do whatever they can to avoid experiencing these memories. The emotional triggers for traumatic memories can include positive, healthy emotions like intimacy and love. Through trial and error, veterans learn that if they don't get too emotionally involved with anything or anyone, they can dramatically reduce the number and intensity of traumatic memories.

You experience symptoms of hyperarousal, such as extreme anxiety, irritability, poor concentration, and insomnia. Trauma-induced memories are created in states of hyperarousal. In the midst of battle or a dangerous mission, a veteran's fight or flight response is working furiously; likewise during the unexpected, horrific scenes that create traumatic memories. When these memories reactivate, so does the veteran's extreme fight or flight response. Unfortunately, the fight or flight response to imminent danger is designed for short bursts—fight the rushing enemy right here and now, or dash off and hide. When this response is reactivated over and over, veterans with PTSD feel the need to be on a constant, heightened state of alert. They can't relax, they can't concentrate on everyday tasks or conversations, and they can't sleep, all because their system is saying don't let your guard down—even though there's no rational need to have one's guard up in the first place.

PTSD is rooted in biology—abnormal memories, which are the sparks of post-traumatic stress, are the result of a particular way in which the brain works. Why is this important? Because it turns out that emotion-based, traumatic memories can be changed into normal, long-term, autobiographical memories. And when this happens, veterans become free of the cause—not just the symptoms—of PTSD.

To understand how this metamorphosis of memory is possible, we need to know how autobiographical memories, the memories with which we're most familiar and aware, are created.

Our Autobiographical Memory System: How the Brain Remembers Our Life Story

Here's an exercise to help illustrate how autobiographical memories form. Try to recall a past event, one you haven't thought about for a long time. You may have gone skiing and met the love of your life. Or you may have gone skiing and broken your arm. The memory can be from when you were six or sixteen, happy or sad, so long as you haven't thought about it in a while.

Got it? Good. Every reader of this book will have an utterly unique, personal memory in mind. Still, they all have one important thing in common: no matter what incident you remembered from the past, it is sure to be one that had a strong emotional impact. It could have been happiness, inspiration, or warmth, or it could have been sadness, sorrow, or anger. Out of the thousand times you walked to elementary school, for instance, you don't remember the ones where nothing happened—you remember the one where Timmy threw a rock at your head, or you found a ten-dollar bill on the sidewalk. The reason is simple. Our brains are hardwired in such a way that we only make long-term memories of events that are emotionally important to us. These autobiographical memories tell us who we are, and the following describes the process by which they form.

In the limbic brain there's a small structure called the amygdala, which is illustrated in the figure below.

Location of the Amygdala in the Brain

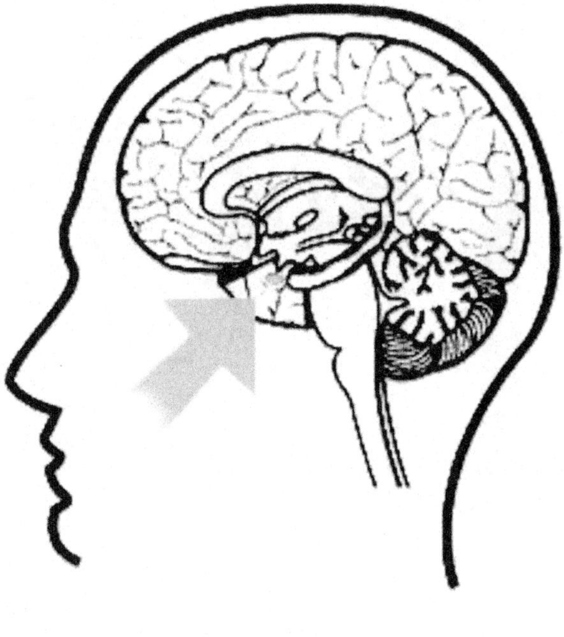

The amygdala, which is activated by strong emotions, tells corresponding structures in the brain to create a memory of that event. The amygdala lights up and tells the brain to store the event's sights, sounds, scents, tastes, and touches, and in a matter of nanoseconds, this information moves from the limbic brain to the human brain. A new, autobiographical memory is formed.

When we experience a traumatizing event, something very different happens (see figure below).

Functional Shut-Down of the Human Brain in Response to a Traumatic Event

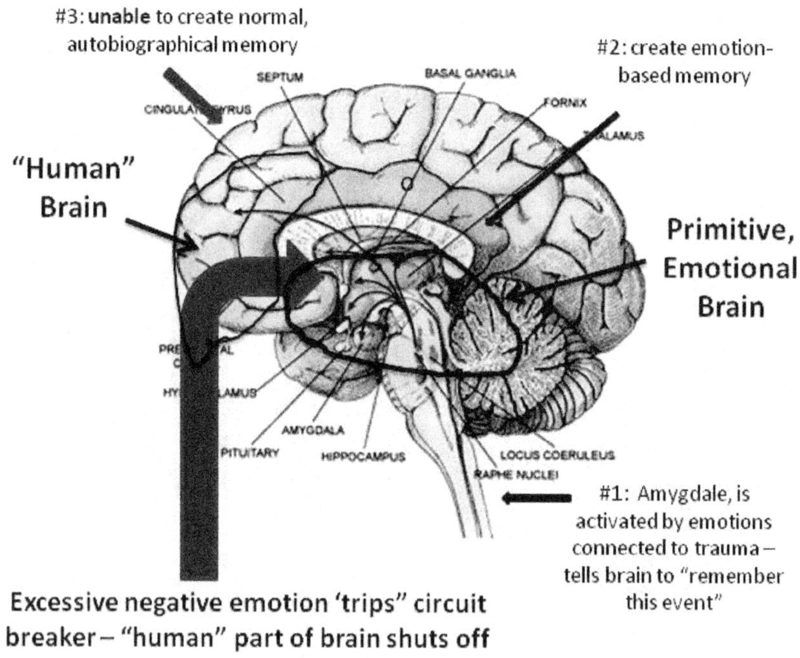

The front, human part of the brain shuts down, unable to complete the third step of the process. This means the memory doesn't get to the part of the brain where it can be recalled at will. The brain works like an incredibly sophisticated computer system. Like computers, the brain has a built-in "circuit breaker" to protect it from the harm of trying to process surges of disturbing emotions. When we experience a traumatizing event, from a biological perspective, the brain blows a fuse. The circuit breaks, and we're left with a partially processed, traumatic memory that can, given the right sensory input, trigger symptoms of post-traumatic stress.

Differences between fully processed memories and trauma-induced, partially processed memories

The difference between fully and partially processed memories is not just a theoretical concept. These memories can actually be seen with specialized brain-imaging techniques. In fact, by using fMRI and radioactive isotopes, researchers have been able to separate partially processed, traumatic memories from fully processed, autobiographical memories.

The differences between the two types of memories fall into four categories: (1) how a memory is activated; (2) how a memory changes in intensity; (3) how a memory is perceived in terms of time; and (4) how a memory is organized. These distinctions are illustrated in the table below.

Differences Between Fully Processed Memories and Trauma-Induced, Limbic Memories

Normal Memories	PTSD memories
Control when we think about them	Triggered involuntarily
With time, emotions feel less and less intense	Intensity of emotion may increase with time
Feel like they happened in the past	Feel like they are happening right now
Linear, organized; parts "fit together" and make sense	Disorganized, overemphasis on details, sensations or emotions

(1) How a Memory is Activated. We choose which autobiographical memories we want to recall, whereas traumatic memories appear suddenly, seemingly at random and without our consent. Some triggers for traumatic memories mimic the traumatic event in obvious ways. Things like fireworks during the Fourth of July or firefights in a war movie can trigger memories of actual war. Other triggers are much more difficult to identify. They can be as subtle as a certain color, a transient feeling, or fleeting scent. Moreover, the limbic brain, where these triggers first register, is much faster than our human brain. It only

takes about 12 milliseconds for our limbic brain to respond to a specific trigger and activate a traumatic memory. It takes more than twice that long for our human brain to even know that it has been triggered. The net effect is that veterans suddenly experience intense fear or anger, and have no logical idea why.

(2) Change in Intensity of Memory. Over time, fully processed memories feel less and less intense. The old adage "time heals" is true when it comes to normal, long-term, autobiographical memories. In the case of traumatic memories, however, the opposite occurs. Over the course of days, weeks, years, and decades, feelings of horror, helplessness, and anxiety stemming from the initial trauma can feel more and more intense. What started as a painful but fleeting burn can build until veterans feel like they're being stabbed in the side with a red-hot branding iron. There are at least three reasons the intensity of these feelings get so much worse over time.

(a) The first is that the psychological "horror" associated with trauma is incapacitating. If veterans felt the full intensity of a traumatic event at the time the event occurred, they'd go into shock. To endure the event with any composure, veterans have no choice but to shut off or compartmentalize compassion. Anyone who has experienced a traumatic event can verify this. You simply have to block it out while it's underway, even though this means you'll be forced to face it later. Thanks to the stress inoculation techniques discussed earlier, the modern soldier is more equipped than ever to compartmentalize his or her compassion in order to accomplish the mission. What they're not trained to do is deal with the psychological fallout of this newfound ability down the road.

(b) The second reason why traumatic memories become more intense over time has to do with the prospect of hope. Once a traumatic event is over, the outcome can't be changed. When the event is actually happening, there's always the slight chance that things aren't as bad as they appear. I know I saw my buddy get shot, but maybe the bullet missed an organ. Maybe he's okay. Hope remains a possibility. A flashback doesn't offer any hope. My buddy got shot, and my buddy died. The fact that there's nothing veterans can do to change what's about to happen (in the flashback) creates feelings of despair, which in turn add to the overall intensity and horror associated with this traumatic memory.

(c) The third reason traumatic memories increase in intensity is that they occur out of context. When or just after veterans experience trauma, they know why they're feeling intense upset or horror—these are painful but appropriate responses to the terrible experiences of war. When veterans are sitting at home watching television or out at a shopping mall and suddenly feel the same way, they have no idea what's happening or why.

(3) <u>Perception of When the Traumatic Event Occurred.</u> We associate memory with events that happened in the past, and that's exactly how fully processed, autobiographical memories feel. If you think about something you did last week, it doesn't feel like it's

happening right now. But that's exactly what happens with abnormal memories of trauma—they make a person feel like the event itself is going on in the present. In the same way you're reading this sentence, trauma-related sounds, scents, tastes, and sights in a flashback seem to be happening at this very moment. Veterans often describe a "split-screen" experience, where the intrusive recollection of something in the past is superimposed over their immediate perception of present reality. This experience throws a person out of whack. It's extremely destabilizing, especially because veterans were never told why this malfunction of memory occurs. The answer is, again, biological.

> Any given perception is the result of millions of bioelectric signals that are reconstructed in the brain to create a representation of the "real" world. There's a very slight delay during this reconstruction, and the brain separates (and stores in different places) the immediate perception from the processed perception (that is, the perception that we recognize consciously). Traumatic memories trigger the immediate data—but the part of the brain that fully processes these memories is never activated. That is, these memories are not put through the circuitry that registers them as having happened in the past. Hence, veterans don't have a way to account for the lapse of time between when an event actually happened and the experience of it happening "right now," brought on by the intrusive memory. This biological delay makes it all the harder to make sense of these intrusive, partially processed memories.

(4) Organization of Memory. Autobiographical memories seem to fit together in logical ways. Even hazy memories are like old, faded photographs. Partially processed, traumatic memories, on the other hand, feel fragmented, disorganized, and just plain strange, like a bunch of random sights, sounds, scents, and tastes all rolled into one. Not all veterans experience this. Some say they remember what happened "all too well." But for many, the memory of a traumatic experience is all the more horrific, because it seems chaotic. It just doesn't make sense. The reason has to do with where the memory is stored, namely, in the limbic brain. Primitive animals like rodents or reptiles do not "think," nor do they remember things the way we do. Research has shown that reptiles "remember" events as a constellation of sights and sounds. The limbic brain functions in much the same way, recording and reproducing sensory data without the proper context to help us understand what these data mean.

Having labored through all this information on the biology of trauma and memory formation, you might ask: Why is this important? The short answer is that, *from the perspective of neuroscience, trauma-induced memories can be changed into autobiographical memories. This, at the very least, should give veterans hope. Even if a veteran has had serious, debilitating PTSD-type symptoms for decades, he or she has the inherent, biological ability to fully process traumatic memories, thus taking the cog out of the vicious cycle that perpetuates symptoms of post-traumatic stress.*

CHAPTER 4

How Trauma Destroys Basic Beliefs

If you fell from the roof and were sure that you'd broken your leg, you'd call the paramedics, your brother, your husband or wife, or your friend for help in getting to the emergency room. Once there, you'd expect doctors and nurses to come to your aid. This course of action, which anyone in an emergency situation would normally follow, relies upon three basic assumptions:

A. Medical professionals (doctors, nurses, paramedics) know a lot more than you do about broken bones and how to fix them.

B. These professionals want to help, are there to help, and will try to help you—and you've come to them because you trust in their ability to fix your broken leg.

C. Fixing the broken bone is going to hurt, and the rehabilitation of your leg will likely be prolonged and painful. Still, it's worth the pain, because you'll ultimately be healthy. Being able to use your leg again to stand up, walk, and run far outweighs the pain and suffering associated with healing.

These assumptions seem so obvious as to not bear mentioning. Of course we only seek out help from those able to provide it, and we wouldn't seek help in the first place if we believed these people really wanted to hurt us or would fail to do us any good. But the truth is that, for most traumatized veterans, these basic assumptions break down. These veterans often believe doctors don't know what they're doing, they don't want to help, and they will cause pain without making things better.

Before a traumatized veteran even talks to a mental health professional, he or she may assume some negative things about the very people who are there to help. They reason:

A. This person can't help me. They don't know me. They weren't with me in the warzone. I know what I suffered better than anyone—what could anyone possibly tell me that I haven't already thought of myself?

B. Asking for help will make everything worse. I've heard of PTSD, and I know buddies who've been diagnosed. If they weren't already screwed up, they were after the doctors got hold of them. I'm not doing that bad, and I'll be damned if I make it worse by talking to a shrink.

C. It's not worth the effort. Say I talk to a psychiatrist—what could they do for me? They'll just try to dope me up with drugs. I can't forget the horrors of what happened to me, and talking with them just reinforces it. No matter what, I'll still be broke, in pain, jobless, homeless, and alone.

You may know—or you may be—a veteran mired in this self-destructive way of thinking. You can find your way out, and the first step is knowing how our lives are grounded by certain basic beliefs, and why we believe these fundamental things to be true.

How Traumatizing Events Destroy a Veteran's Basic Beliefs

We take certain beliefs for granted. Let's call these "basic beliefs," fundamental ways in which we experience the world, and what we expect to happen to us as a result.

Consider your belief in gravity. In your everyday experience you have no reason to question this "law"—I'm holding a pen, I let it go, the pen falls. Or: I'm approaching a cliff. I stop at the edge, because if I took another step, I'd tumble down. We walk around, lift things up, feel their weight, set them down, and hop, skip, and jump without ever giving gravity a second thought. We've just come to know from experience that gravity's there, it's working, and we have no reason to think that it will go away. The same is true for dozens of other basic beliefs. But we have to understand something: We hold these beliefs because experience tells us that these beliefs hold true. While science, logic, and reason may prove Newton's law of gravity, it's not logic but the past experience of falling or seeing things fall that keeps you from wandering over the cliff.

To take this point further, imagine that, without warning, you and the table, chairs, forks, and spoons at your dinner table started to float up in the air. You watch in awe for two seconds—then you and the rest come crashing down. Now imagine how you'd feel in this shocking, short-lived scenario. You'd freak out, or freeze, or yell, "What the hell just happened?" What's worse, you'd start to worry about when gravity might fail again, and when it might randomly re-engage and send everything crashing down on your head.

Someone who is 30 years old has lived for almost one billion seconds. From the perspective of science, two seconds out of a billion is not worth mentioning. It's an anomaly, and logic says it shouldn't matter. But your experience says something very different. Your basic belief in gravity has been shaken. The same thing can happen with deployment-related events, and this fuels the confusion of a traumatized veteran.

Other things can seem "true" simply by logic or nature, but actually feel "true" because of experience (or lack thereof). Take for example, most children, who take it as truth that they're invincible. Being so young, experience has not yet taught the average child that certain actions can result in death; they're still orienting themselves to the idea of danger. So by an adult's standard, jumping from a high ledge into a pool of water is illogical, crazy, irresponsible, and immensely dangerous; from the child's point of view, it's fun and exciting, consequences be damned. Furthermore, no amount of reasoning or talking with a child will totally curtail such behavior—that is, you can't convince the child to give up on danger using logic, no matter how rational and airtight your argument is. Later into life, teenagers assume that if something unexpected and potentially life-threatening were to happen, they would be able to "figure something out," some action or evasive response that would keep them and their loved ones safe. This belief is not based on logic; the teenage mind just assumes it to be true. It's like at any given instant they can summon a magical shield to save them from harm.

Another basic belief we develop from infancy assumes that the people who care about us will keep us safe. This belief is also rooted in the experience of children who are fortunate enough to grow up with compassionate parents or guardians who protected them. As infants, their caregivers fed them, changed their diapers, and made sure they were warm enough at night. As toddlers, strong hands would keep them afloat in a pool or steady them as they walked across an icy sidewalk. Millions of these experiences teach children, in a very deep and basic way, the following: People who are in charge care about you, and will do everything they can to keep you out of harm's way.

Children innately assume that the world is a benign, wonderful place, a playground that he or she can enjoy and explore. Children don't think about this logically. These ideas start long before they can talk, or even form a complete thought. They just "know" it's true, and to a large extent this truth is carried forward with us into adulthood; it's essential to our interactions with other people and ideas in the world we engage in as adults.

Trauma can change this, and the results are profound. When veterans are traumatized, one or all of these basic beliefs are destroyed, at least for a time. As a result, veterans now intuitively feel something like the following:

A. I am basically incompetent. I know something really, really bad will happen, and when it does, I can't depend on myself to save myself or others.

B. I can't trust other people. No matter what they say or do, other people are selfish at their core; given the chance, they'll take advantage of me and sell me out for their own gain.

C. The world is a meaningless place. Why should I get excited about anything when in the end it's probably not going to work; even if I try as hard as I can at something, things will be just as bad as they were before.

Some veterans assume that these beliefs are logical, and that there is no rational alternative to feeling so pessimistically about the world or other human beings. Hence, any attempt to accept or do good in the world seems inherently false; it goes against logic. What veterans need to learn is how to rehabilitate the basic beliefs that got them through so many tough times before. And this requires a major leap of faith: a commitment to act in ways consistent with prior, pre-trauma, experience-based, basic beliefs. Basic beliefs may be wrecked by trauma, but they can be rebuilt.

CHAPTER 5

Killing Compassion: Military Culture and PTSD

If you saw your friend with his arm in a sling, you'd naturally ask, "What happened to your arm?" But if your friend was diagnosed with PTSD, you'd never ask, "What happened to your head?" Still, it's natural to want to know "why." After all, lots of soldiers have been deployed, and not all develop PTSD. It's normal for people close to the veteran to ask, "Why you?" and for veterans themselves to ask, "Why me?"

The trouble is that PTSD, like all mental health diagnoses, is a very sensitive issue, and the question of "why" often implies fault or weakness. Since PTSD carries this negative stigma, questions about it become taboo. Unfortunately, this has been especially true in military culture.

PTSD is a psychiatric illness, and therefore subject to a well-known and pervasive stigma against individuals who suffer from it. Commanders may discourage their soldiers from seeking mental-health therapy when they think it will be detrimental to a soldier's capacity to fight. Soldiers are told to suck it up, stay tough, and not admit to any problems with their mental health. They may be told that seeking help or going to a mental health professional would revoke their security clearance, or simply end their military career. Sometimes the message is as simple as this: if a soldier needs medication for mental health issues, they're of no value to their unit. For any soldier dedicated to serving God and country, that's a devastating thing to hear.

Things have gotten better in recent years. An official motto has arisen that says, "It takes the strength and courage of a warrior to ask for help." Generals and other high-ranking officials can be seen on talk shows and media interviews openly talking about post-deployment psychological hardships faced by their soldiers or themselves. The military certainly seems to be stepping up its efforts to encourage more service members to seek help for post-traumatic stress. But many are still left in the dark, and we have a long way to go toward bringing the discussion of PTSD into the light.

Of course, mental health-related stigma is pervasive outside of the military as well. Many people continue to believe that only "weak-minded" people develop problems such as depression, drug dependency, or PTSD. But this is simply untrue. In fact, only strong, healthy, compassionate people develop PTSD. Here's why.

One thing we need to understand is how PTSD fits into the array of mental health diagnoses. You may have heard of someone with a "pathological" tendency. "Pathological" means "indicative of a disease." Say someone steals a loaf of bread because his son would otherwise starve. Or a woman lies about helping hide a battered friend so as not to put her in danger. However we feel about the act of stealing or lying, there are reasons, arguably very good reasons, for such acts in certain circumstances. When someone is a pathological thief or liar, however, they lie or steal without having a reason—they perform these acts compulsively, because they have some inner drive that pushes them to do so, as if a disease creates the need to make bad choices.

PTSD is an extremely serious, potentially life-threatening condition, but it is not a sign of pathology. Only veterans who are normal, compassionate human beings, and who perform their military service to the best of their abilities can become traumatized. In every case, veterans become traumatized because they cared—they cared about a buddy who was maimed or killed, or about the civilian who lost life or limb. Veterans also care about themselves—they want to stay alive, not die on the field of battle. Put simply, if a veteran had lacked compassion for him or herself, or others, they would not have been traumatized, and they could not have gotten PTSD.

TRAINING SOLDIERS TO KILL BY TRAINING THEM TO CARE

To be traumatized, three things have to be true. **First**, something awful, horrific, and life-threatening occurs—a schoolroom is blown up by a suicide bomber. **Second**, this event was unexpected, causing an intense feeling of shock—the schoolroom was outside the official warzone and in no perceived danger before the sudden explosion. **Third**, you have to care about the people involved—that is, care about the loss of innocent, young lives, or a specific person to whom you were personally connected. Unless all three conditions are true, a person won't become traumatized.

There are many people in the world who lack compassion for their fellow human beings. They don't care about doing good for others, and they don't feel bad when others suffer harm. Clinically, we call these people sociopaths, and in the military, sociopaths are an extremely dangerous liability. Make no mistake, the military wants soldiers who can kill, and it trains them to become better killers. But it also trains soldiers to have compassion for their own troops, and to draw from that compassion as a source to become more fierce and indomitable in battle. A cold-blooded, sociopathic killer who lacks compassion for anyone else would just as soon shoot his or her own soldiers as kill the enemy. Sociopaths are dangerous, uncontrollable—and no military commander wants one in their unit. Hence, one of the military's primary goals in training is to encourage service members to care about one another—and for good reason. When you're under threat in a battle situation, and you care about saving your buddy's life as much as your own, you're a much more valuable soldier.

Of course, the military does not use emotionally charged words like "caring" and "compassion." Military culture is hard, and these words are soft. Terms like "group cohesion," "espres de corps," and "allegiance to core military values" work better, but the intent is the same: engrain the feeling that service members are like family. You'd sooner die than do nothing while you watch them suffer.

The military's rationale is clear. The historian, S.L. A. Marshall first reported on the combat effectiveness of World War II units as the result of training that encouraged "brotherhood." Contemporary studies on the effectiveness of units in the current Global War on Terror show that compassionate soldiers make the best killers.

Read that again: Compassionate soldiers make the best killers[5]. And together these compassionate individuals form the tightest, most devastatingly effective combat units. This may seem like a contradiction, but it's been proven true. In conflict after conflict, the most difficult warriors to defeat are those fighting for their land, their family, or their children. Historian SLA Marshall wrote in *Men Against Fire*[6]:

> I hold it to be one of the simplest truths of war that the thing which enables an infantry soldier to keep going with his weapons is the near presence or the presumed presence of a comrade ... He is sustained by his fellows primarily and by his weapons secondarily.

Compassion, however, comes at a high price, and the emotional debt can hit veterans years, or even decades, after their military service has ended. Unfortunately, compassionate people are sometimes put in situations where they are asked to do non-compassionate things—to make a sacrifice, or to endanger or harm innocents. The coexistence of compassion and cold-heartedness in a soldier makes him or her a deadlier weapon in war. But the conflict between these emotions outside of battle is what leads to PTSD.

SHEEP, WOLVES AND SHEEPDOGS: THREE ROLES AMONG CIVILIANS AND SOLDIERS

In the book *On Killing*, LTC Dave Grossman presents three types of people: sheep, wolves, and sheepdogs. Sheep represent individuals who are predominantly compassionate, people who are kind, empathetic, and care deeply for others and themselves, but lack the ability to intentionally hurt or kill other people. When faced with exceptional stress, such as live fire or bodily injury, such people can become immobile, unable to act.

Wolves represent the polar opposite. Wolves can act coldly, without compassion or remorse for the hurt they cause others. They can also kill without a second thought. In this sense, wolves can be thought of as sociopaths, the cold-blooded killers referred to before: wholly self-interested and therefore dangerous to friends as well as enemies who get in their way.

Sheepdogs are a kind of hybrid, having the qualities of both sheep and wolves, as well as the capacity to use these qualities to the advantage of themselves or others. Like wolves, sheepdogs can intentionally take a life and continue to function under extreme duress. The difference is that they do so while still caring deeply about themselves and others. For sheepdogs, the capacity to kill is driven by the deeply felt need to protect.

Normal, high-functioning service members are sheepdogs. Their compassion motivates them to fight, and their wolf-like warrior instinct enables them to do whatever's necessary in combat. Sheepdog warriors can shut down the sheep-like instinct for care and compassion during the heat of battle. Sheepdogs care about their fellow soldiers, and that care drives them to keep those soldiers and themselves alive in battle. But—and this is the key point—sheepdogs can cancel out the care and compassion that would force them to feel the full intensity and horror of what they saw, touched, smelled, and heard on the battlefield. If soldiers/warriors/sheepdogs couldn't do this, they would become overwhelmed with the emotions that compassion for others lets us feel; they would freeze up, unable to pull the trigger when life is on the line.

Soldiers who do freeze up like this are called victims of "combat fatigue," and they are referred to a Combat Stress Control unit to help them recover. Still, such instances are relatively rare. According to a study released by the UK, only four out of 46,000 troops sent to Iraq in 2003 as part of Operation Iraqi Freedom had to be evacuated out due to psychological problems resulting from their experience in combat[7]—that's less than one in ten thousand soldiers. This low figure is a testament to how well-trained today's service members are. Their training exercises use live rounds and explosives. They're trained to use muscle memory to "shoot first, think later." In effect, this training serves two purposes. First, it helps ensure missions go as planned—only unexpected, horrific events can cause PTSD, and thorough training reduces the likelihood of the unexpected. Second, repeated, realistic training scenarios make service members better at "compartmentalizing" the compassionate part of themselves, when necessary, in order to continue to function.

Traumatized veterans don't have to reengage the compassionate part of their brains when they return from deployment, but can continue to function, at a certain level, in "warrior" mode. With their warrior instincts still active and dominant, veterans can go to college or trade school. They can gain jobs and make a path toward a career. They can get married and raise a family. But in warrior mode, veterans can't afford to become overly passionate about anything or anyone, because they know almost by instinct that to do so would risk creating a very serious, even life-threatening problem for themselves. As a result, many veterans avoid experiencing any feelings of intense joy or happiness. It's emotionally safer, they think, to keep these feelings in check.

The trouble is that such experiences of intense, positive emotions are directly connected to a person's compassion for himself and others. As long as a traumatized veteran can keep strong emotions at bay, it's possible that his or her compassionate impulses will keep quiet, too. But inevitably—though it may take years or even decades—the need for emotional, compassionate human connections breaks through. And it's when this compassionate impulse returns that traumatized veterans risk activating partially processed traumatic memories. It's as if these memories are seeds that have been lying dormant during a seemingly endless winter. When the sunshine and gentle rains of spring at last arrive, these seeds wake up, sprout, and shoot into the warmth and light. Many veterans, however, are not prepared for this "cropping up," and the realization of all these unaccounted memories—and the feeling that you're responsible for them—can be too much to bear. Veterans can go for very long spans in warrior mode with minimal or no PTSD symptoms. Then they lower their defenses, they retire, they have grandchildren, and "boom"—out of nowhere come tortured flashbacks from a 40-year-old war. This is the story behind countless reoccurrences of trauma among Vietnam vets. Without intervention, it's bound to cause suffering to veterans of our more recent conflicts overseas.

The good news is that even veterans with chronic PTSD symptoms can learn essential skills to help them recover their compassion for—and their capacity for trust and closeness with—themselves and others. They just need a plan, and the help of a community of professionals, friends, and family to help them see it through.

CHAPTER 6

Unintended Effects - How We Talk about the Problem of PTSD

One of the biggest challenges in helping veterans recover from post-traumatic stress is getting them to show up for their first appointment. As discussed in the previous chapter, veterans with PTSD frequently feel ashamed, embarrassed, or guilty about having been diagnosed with this "psychiatric illness." Moreover, they take PTSD symptoms as a sign that they're "losing it," that they're weak or defective, or that they're just going crazy. Psychiatric treatments for PTSD can and do work, but most veterans aren't in a position to know of—or believe in—the benefits of therapy. To put veterans in a position to heal, we need to help them re-conceptualize the problem. Let's start with three misconceptions that have fueled the negative, treatment-discouraging stigma against PTSD.

Reversing the negative spin on mental health

To diagnose and treat mental health problems, psychiatrists rely on a work called the *Diagnostic and Statistical Manual for Psychiatric Diagnosis*—better known as the

DSM-IV-TR. This official textbook describes all known psychiatric conditions, including PTSD. There's a sense that the names of the conditions themselves—General Anxiety Disorder, Panic Disorder, Social Phobia—are negative, and so are symptoms like excessive sweating, nervous twitches, and an awkwardness around other people.

Well, of course they're negative, you might say. These disorders and their symptoms indicate a problem. But that doesn't mean the only way to define a disorder is with negative connotations or by suggesting a person is somehow "screwed up in the head." To get some perspective on this, think about the following situation: You see a child hitting other children on the playground. Is your first thought this child has a serious mental illness? Probably not. Instead, we assume that the child simply doesn't know any better way to conduct himself, or that his conduct is wrong. The child needs to learn new, better, constructive ways of dealing with anger or aggression. It is the same thing with the "new kid" who doesn't play with others. Is she clinically depressed or just painfully shy? If a child really is psychologically impaired, medication may be the best means of controlling his or her behavior. But if he simply doesn't know the etiquette of the schoolyard, the "rules" of proper play, then an example-led, hands-on education in social skills is a far better way to approach the problem.

The same situation applies to veterans with PTSD, who may act out or withdraw in ways that make those around them think, *What's wrong?* It's extremely important that we learn to define the problem differently so that negative perceptions of PTSD, and mental health disorders in general, don't skew our opinions on how to help sufferers of post-traumatic stress. PTSD is a serious mental illness, and medications, in addition to other treatment methods, can be effective, responsible approaches to the problem. But at its core, veterans don't need chemicals to counter symptoms of PTSD. They need, like the overly aggressive or shy child, to become re-accustomed to normal society's "rules of play." They need, in essence, to learn specific skills that will allow them to experience life again as members of their families, communities, places of work, and society at large.

As we discussed earlier, having PTSD doesn't mean a person is crazy or pathological. Many symptoms of PTSD are, in fact, familiar to any effective soldier: quick reflexes, hyperawareness, and the ability to suppress strong emotions that could cripple one's ability to fight. PTSD symptoms are the normal, expected, healthy response to abnormal, unexpected, traumatizing events. These symptoms only become a problem when they don't decrease in intensity over time, allowing the sufferer to recover to the state he or she was in before the trauma occurred.

Post-deployment mental health problems have been acknowledged for centuries. Labeled everything from "soldier's heart" to "combat neurosis," these diagnoses share one assumption: normal, healthy, well-adjusted individuals don't suffer long-term problems from exposure to the horrors of war. The perception, however, began to change in the wake of the Vietnam War, when literally hundreds of thousands of returning veterans were the subjects of the harshest kind of social condemnation. There was a "blame the victim"[8] mentality in place with respect to veterans succumbing to mental disorders after coming home from war. The mental health establishment, encouraged by some prominent, pioneering researchers, led the fight to create a new psychiatric diagnosis that didn't blame veterans for their long-term, post-conflict psychological problems. In 1980, Post-Traumatic Stress Disorder entered the books as an official diagnosis, one that would help veterans make progress in a reality apart from that of war.

The new mantra said that PTSD was the result of a "normal response to abnormal events." In short, the theory states that any person can only deal with so much psychological stress. When this stress hits hard and/or lasts long, we all hit a breaking point, and the result is a serious and often long-term psychiatric problem. Studies have shown that prolonged combat can kill or maim the mind as much as the body. A study from WWII found that 98% of soldiers who spent more than 60 consecutive days in combat became psychiatric casualties[9]. The remaining 2%, it's important to state, were determined to have pre-existing, "aggressive psychopathic personalities." This means that virtually every soldier who was not already psychologically impaired suffered permanent psychological damage as a result of intense, prolonged experience in battle. It's studies like these that have helped turn the tide from blaming veterans for being "weak-minded" to seeing the gears of war churn out psychiatric casualties without discretion. More recent, scientific studies by Breslau, and others, done in the 1980s, further served to confirm these assumptions.[10]

There's trouble, however, in shifting the blame for PTSD from soldiers to war itself. The shift can imply that veterans are powerless—that they can't help but fall victim to the mental disorder, and that the only way out is through a permanent regimen of drugs and outside intervention. But the fact is that friends and family can help veterans recover, and veterans have enormous power to help themselves.

SYMPTOMS VS. CAUSES OF PTSD

The focus on the symptoms vs. the causes of PTSD has resulted in treatments for the disorder—that is, relief from some of its harshest effects—but not a proper cure, which would mean release from the disorder itself. Let's say your hand hurts and you have no idea why. You take a couple aspirin and your hand stops hurting. But are you "cured?" Once the aspirin wears off, or your hand goes from rest to duty, the pain returns. It might be that the skin's irritated by the soap you use to wash the car. Maybe the tendons are stressed by too much typing or shoveling. Maybe the bones are suffering from a condition only a doctor could diagnose. Pain relievers can help you feel better in each case, but the underlying cause rages on.

This is a crucial thing to understand. If treatments fail to cure PTSD—and PTSD, as a disorder, is largely assumed to be altogether incurable—then veterans are put in a position where the best way to deal with PTSD is to avoid being diagnosed with it. And avoidance can have disastrous results.

The military's current stance concerning PTSD is grounded in prevention. The intent is to make service members more resilient to the effects of combat-related traumatic events, a sort of vaccination against the onset of PTSD. We immunize children against specific, potentially life-threating diseases with low, harmless doses of the very "bug" that in higher doses could result in severe illness or death. A child's body reacts to this false "infection" by building immunity, becoming stronger, so that if the child does "catch a bug", she can fight it and win. To replicate this preventative process with service members, the military employs a practice called "stress inoculation training."

The military "inoculates" soldiers to the effects of PTSD by putting them through realistic, stressful role-playing scenarios that mimic, with increasing intensity, the events of war. The U.S. Marines' RAPTOR (Research, Assessment, Performance, Training Optimization and Resilience) program epitomizes this approach to combat readiness, putting combat forces under extreme combat-like conditions until they're considered immune to the pressure. After a certain amount of exposure to simulated war horrors, it's assumed a soldier will not flinch from the real thing. He or she is resilient, impregnable, "tough as nails" when it comes to trauma. On the other end of the spectrum, soldiers lack resilience, and it's these soldiers who end up with chronic, debilitating PTSD. The chart below illustrates traits from each end of the resiliency spectrum from green ("Ready") to red ("Ill").

Unfortunately, this desensitization approach to PTSD is fundamentally limited. While it helps strengthen a soldier's resolve to fight, it can't completely inoculate a soldier against the effects of trauma. The approach is even potentially dangerous. Many, many veterans actually develop chronic PTSD symptoms as a result of the military training that is designed to prevent them. There's a very fine line between training a service member in how to encounter future trauma, and just traumatizing a service member in the course of that very training. As we discussed in Chapter 4, unexpected traumatic events shatter service members' experiential (experience-based) basic

The Stress Continuum Model[11]

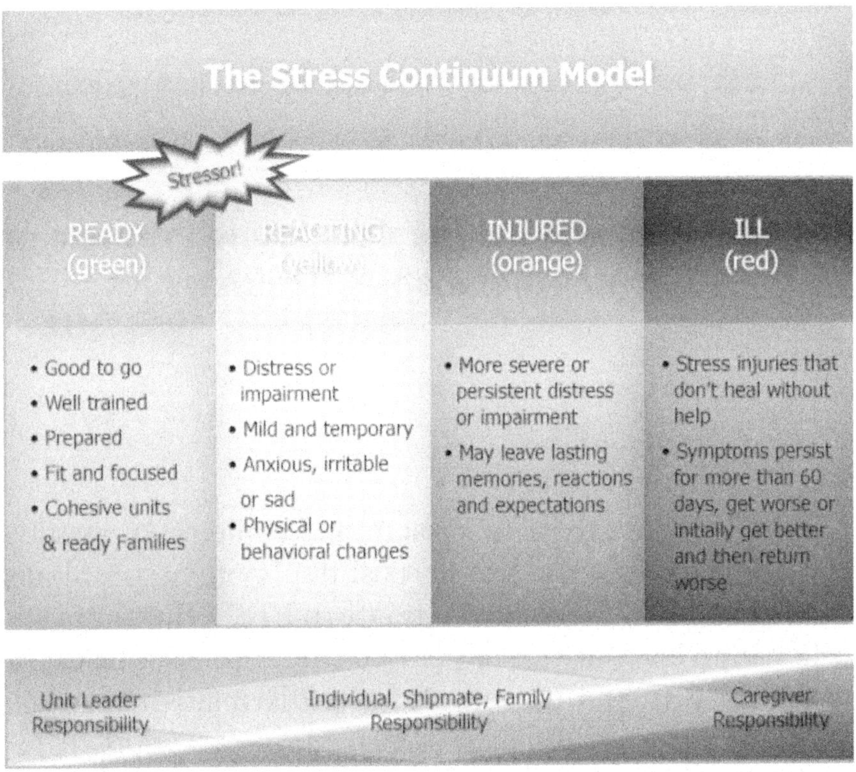

beliefs about themselves, others and the world. It's very difficult to create training scenarios that simply dent, versus utterly destroy, these beliefs. The military plays its part in preparing soldiers for battle; it's up to veterans and veteran helpers to understand how PTSD develops and what measures they can take to recover once they've returned from their deployment.

CHAPTER 7

The Snowball Effect - The Compound Problem of PTSD and other Mental Health Issues

PTSD doesn't exist in a vacuum. People often assume that all post-combat or post-deployment problems having to do with the brain equate to PTSD. But there are other injuries that can happen to the brain as a result of action in war, and it's important to distinguish between these and post-traumatic stress. Many veterans, especially those deployed to the current conflicts in Iraq and Afghanistan, suffer traumatic brain injuries, have chronic pain, have other deployment-related medical problems, are abusing alcohol or other illegal substances, and have unresolved traumatic grief. We also have to look at how PTSD and other conditions can co-occur, because by the time a veteran comes for treatment for PTSD, he or she may be suffering from a myriad of other stressors.

Three of the most common of these co-occurring conditions—process addiction, traumatic brain injury, and unresolved traumatic grief—are described below.

Process Addictions

The modern world is full of people, things, and situations that can make us anxious, irritable, and highly stressed out. Unfortunately, for many veterans with PTSD, feelings of intolerable anxiety, anger, or grief often manifest themselves, putting veterans on edge. Understandably, veterans want to find ways to lower stress levels to get rid of these extremely unpleasant feelings, and they generally do so in one of two ways:

1. By doing something that relieves intolerable feelings in the short term and is in the veteran's best long-term interests, or;
2. By doing something that relieves intolerable feelings in the short term, but that is not in the veteran's best long-term interests.

The first route can be described as healthy, but the second cannot. Healthy routines include activities like talking with other people, playing sports, or going for a walk or a hike. Unhealthy routines for dealing with stress include drinking, or even exercising in excess, as a distraction from intolerable feelings of anxiety, anger, or grief. Such actions can create relief in the short term, but there's little benefit to them over the long term when it comes to recovery from stress, let alone PTSD.

Alcohol abuse and other addictions are called "process addictions" when they're done more for the process and not so much for the goal. In other words, a process addiction is a dependency to a mood-altering behavior done for the purpose, to put it simply, of doing something. This behavior becomes a welcome distraction from everyday worries, but again, only for a short while. Cornered by stressful circumstances and desperately wanting to feel better, a person turns to a process for a way out. They're controlled by a desperate need to escape, and like a hamster on a wheel, the compulsive act gives them a sense of distracted accomplishment, though there's no escape in sight.

TRAUMATIC BRAIN INJURY

Traumatic brain injuries (TBIs), often the result of blasts from Improvised Explosive Devices (IEDs), have been called the "signature" wound of the current conflicts in Iraq and Afghanistan. Improvements to vehicular and body armor have allowed countless soldiers to survive explosions that would otherwise have killed them. But the intense detonation of an IED does tremendous damage to the brain, jerking the head and neck back and forth like a ragdoll on a string.

Interestingly enough, from both a clinical and neuroscience perspective, it is often difficult to differentiate between which symptoms are primarily due to a traumatic brain injury and which ones are due primarily to PTSD. From the perspective of neuroscience, it's difficult to distinguish between symptoms of TBI and PTSD. For example, in 2007, Dr. Hoge and colleagues found that in veterans who had a traumatic brain injury, only headaches and elevated pulse, reliably differentiates between this two conditions[12].

But TBIs are physical and PTSD is psychological, you might say, so how can their symptoms be so similar?

There are three reasons:
First - **The same injuries that cause traumatic brain injury can also cause PTSD.** Blast injuries, such as from an IED (improvised exploding devises) which cause head injuries in combat are, by definition, an unexpected life-threatening event; one where either the service member, or those he or she cares about, could have been seriously injured or killed. This is a classic example of the type of event that can lead to PTSD.

Second - **Independent of the direction of the explosion, the same parts of the brain biologically altered by PTSD are damaged by concussive explosions**[13]. This can best be understood by remembering that the brain is basically like a balloon tethered inside of a larger balloon (skull). When hit from any direction, the brain tends to first hit forward (called a "coup") and then hit backwards (a "contrecoup"), as illustrated below.

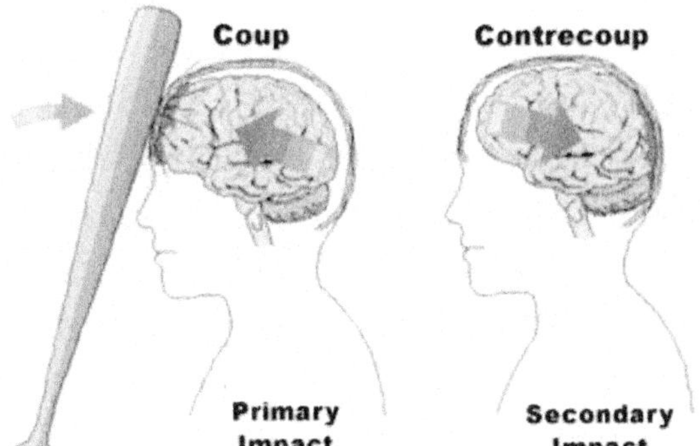

It's also important to note that most of the inside of the skull is smooth. Only a few areas, including those areas directly in front of the limbic brain that are responsible for the creation of emotional memories, are pointy, as shown in the figure below.

Sagittal (cross-sectional) view of inside of a human skull

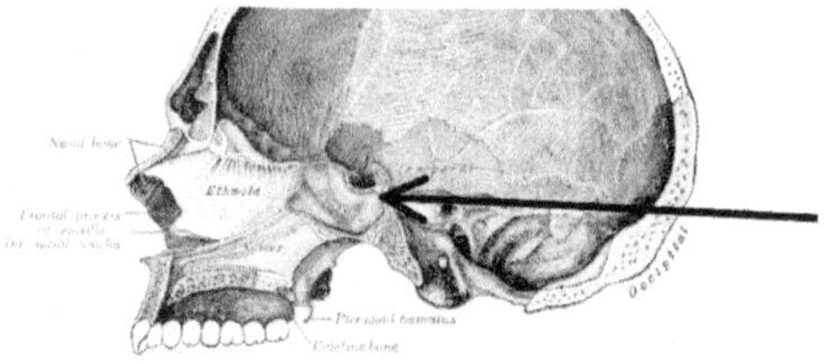

Sphenoid process – two bat shaped, pointy bones that "stick out" of the bottom, front part of the skull

Whether a veteran is hit from the back or the front, the violent rocking motion the brain endures inside the skull causes damage to both parts of the brain. Hence, independent of the mechanism of injury, because of how the brain is tethered and the position inside of the skull that is not smooth, traumatic brain injuries can have the same or similar effects on the brain as do psychological injuries such as PTSD.

Three - **Cellular regeneration and regrowth (neurogenesis) is important in the etiology of both TBI and PTSD.** People tend to assume that Traumatic Brain Injuries are physical injuries, while PTSD is primarily a psychological process. However, interestingly enough, on a cellular level, the two conditions are almost indistinguishable[14]. In both TBI and PTSD, a specific area of the brain called the dendrite nucleus (which is an integral part of the emotional memory system) is physically damaged. Recovery occurs by a process called neurogenesis—a process by which nerves that have been damaged regenerate as well as make important new connections to surrounding cells and neurons. However, in both PTSD and TBI, this process does not always occur, which results in the cognitive deficits often seen in both conditions. More importantly, each condition makes the other one more difficult to recover from[15].

UNRESOLVED TRAUMATIC GRIEF

Traumatic grief is a condition that affects even more returning combat veterans than PTSD, and many clinicians and researchers talk about PTSD as if it includes all the symptoms of traumatic grief. There is a great deal of symptom overlap between these two conditions, as shown in the Venn diagram below:

Symptoms Overlap Between PTSD and Traumatic Grief

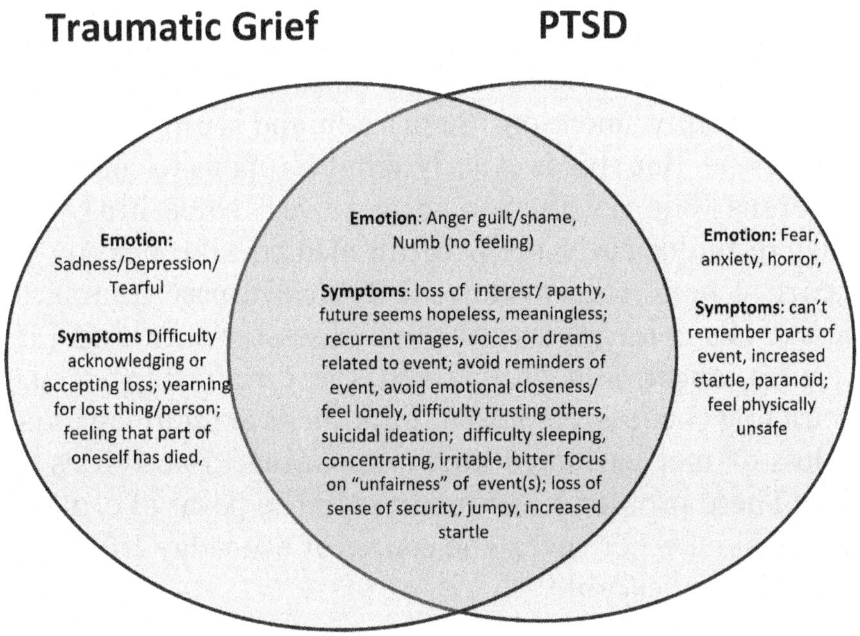

But there are important differences as well. PTSD affects feelings about the future; feelings that something bad will happen sometime soon or down the road; these feelings are characterized as fear or anxiety. Traumatic grief, by contrast, produces feelings of sadness or shame about an event that is past. Most importantly, traumatic grief stems from a loss that is permanent. When a loved one, a friend, a child or a fellow soldier dies, they're gone forever.

The focus for any active member of the military is on the present and the future. The past matters only insofar as learning from past actions can make present and future actions more effective. Grieving involves talking about and doing things with others that were connected to what was lost—that is, connected to the past. Examples include attending a funeral, building a memorial, or establishing a fund in honor of a person who has died. In the military, a special memorial event may involve the entire company or battalion. These ceremonies can be moving and powerful, but for many grieving veterans they're not enough. Imagine if you lost your child and were allowed to mourn for only one day before you were told to simply "move on." Such a demand is unreasonable, even cruel. But this is exactly what happens to countless veterans who try in vain to "get over" something that they're biologically pre-programmed to take heavily to heart. When veterans don't fully grieve past traumatic losses, the consequences include obsessive thinking, bitterness, anger, and guilt about the circumstances surrounding the loss; emotional numbness, detachment, and a loss of motivation to pursue meaningful activities in life. These problems can progress to the point of clinical depression, where even the course of everyday life itself becomes unbearable.

You may recall these three consequences as some of the most serious symptoms of PTSD, and there's a central takeaway here. The combination of PTSD, Process Addiction, Traumatic Brain Injury and/or unresolved traumatic grief greatly increases the risk that veterans will consider, attempt, and actually succeed at killing themselves.

CHAPTER 8

PTSD, Veterans and Suicide

Suicide is as serious as it gets when it comes to the possible consequences of post-traumatic stress. The relationship between exposure to repeated traumatic events in combat, and the increasing number of suicide attempts and successful suicides from veterans of Operation Enduring Freedom (OEF) and Operation Iraqi Freedom (OIF), is all but undeniable. The media has focused a lot of attention on the issue of suicide in returning OEF and OIF veterans, and for good reason. The number of deployed National Guardsmen who took their own lives more than doubled from 2008 to 2009. According to official military estimates, the number of hospitalizations with a primary diagnosis of "suicidal ideation," the clinical term for attempting to kill oneself, increased more than 7,000% between 2006 and 2010. It's estimated that 10 to 15% of deployed veterans will consider suicide. Fortunately, most will not make the attempt. Unfortunately, the majority don't get the help they need to deal with suicidal thoughts, especially when they're recurrent. These veterans suffer, potentially for decades, unaware that they have a treatable, predictable consequence of their exposure to combat-related trauma.

The connection between deployment-related trauma and suicide can be summarized as follows:

#1 Deployment-related trauma can cause veterans to feel emotionally disconnected from their friends, families, and fellow veterans. Trauma can also cause veterans to assume that they're incapable of ever re-connecting.

#2 The combination of feeling disconnected and the sense that a veteran is fundamentally flawed can cause the veteran to consider suicide.

#3 An inadvertent side effect of combat training is that veterans increase their capacity to kill themselves—that is, they develop a fearlessness of death, without which they couldn't take their own lives.

To kill oneself, a person needs both the capacity to do so as well as the desire to die. Between training for combat and experiencing trauma while deployed, combat veterans are inadvertently "primed", given the right circumstances, to end their lives. The result is an epidemic of suicide attempts, completed suicides, and quasi-suicidal behavior, such as "death by cop", driving recklessly, and acting extremely belligerent while drunk.

Human Connections and the Biological Need to Bond

Suicide is never a decision based on reason. When someone chooses to end his or her own life, it's not because they wish to die. It's rather because of an overwhelming need to end unbearable psychological suffering. The origin of this suffering is neither rational nor conscious, but rather the unintentional impediment of one of our most basic psychological needs—the need to emotionally connect with other people, the world, and ourselves. These connections are literally life-sustaining. Emotionally, people can make it through "hell and back" when they're sustained by close human connections. On the other hand, if we feel we've lost the capacity to deeply connect with something outside of ourselves, our emotional health begins to deteriorate. We feel disconnected, disoriented. Just as emotional connections enrich and sustain life, the lack of them robs life of meaning, leading people in these desperate straits to lose the will to live. Dr. Edwin S. Shneidman, a pioneer in the study of suicide, calls this experience "psychache"—a prolonged, seemingly interminable experience of psychological or emotional pain[16]. Besieged by psychache, many war-torn veterans may consider suicide as a way out.

The human need to connect with other people is innate and emotionally essential. Our bodies work to connect with other humans from the moment we're born. Researchers[17] in Sweden identified a specific, coordinated hand/mouth sequence in newborns when placed near the mother's breast. As the babies suckled, they also massaged to maximize the mother's release of oxytocin, a hormone known to intensify feelings of emotional connectedness in post-partum mothers. The need and capacity to emotionally connect is intuitive, and the experience of a normal, emotionally connected upbringing has engrained this in the body and mind. It's part of our biological constitution; a way we're given by nature to feel.

On the other hand, when an upbringing is traumatic or deprives someone of the opportunities to connect with others, things go wrong. In a classic experiment, Hungarian psychiatrist Dr. Rene Spitz studied the effects of maternal separation in the early life of a child[18]. He found that infants who had been separated from their mothers and sent to an orphanage, where their physical needs were met but their emotional needs were left wanting, experienced a sequence of increasingly severe behavioral and emotional disturbances. These infants became withdrawn and suffered from sleeplessness, weight loss, agitation, and hindered physical and psychological development. The medical literature refers to this condition as "failure to thrive." In the worst cases, infants in the study became physically rigid. Some died. Adults can suffer the same fate. Individuals with extremely severe depression can develop a syndrome called catatonia, which makes a person so physically rigid and emotionally detached that they can barely move or speak. Without medical intervention, this condition can be fatal.

Denial and the Breakdown of Emotional Connectivity

Fortunately, both catatonia and failure to thrive are rare—again, because our need to connect in meaningful ways with other people and share ideals is so persistent and powerful that it takes a massive, overarching tidal wave of trauma to break this need down. Unfortunately, veterans are often made to bear the brunt of this traumatic wave during and after tours of duty. Veterans who experience deployment-related trauma often feel the same way that New Yorkers felt in the hours and days after 9/11—that is, on a perpetual, unhinged verge of terror. As visceral as traumatic events are, it can be hard to believe that they actually happened. For veterans who saw, heard, smelled, tasted, touched, and participated in a traumatic event (versus seeing or reading about it from afar), this partial state of unreality, the false feeling of hope that maybe the traumatic event never really happened, can last months, years, even decades. Moreover, this feeling compounds feelings that veterans are emotionally disconnected from others and that they are incompetent, helpless, and unable to improve their situation. And this hopelessness, the feeling that a person is a burden on the present and that the future holds no promise, is one of the key factors in suicide.

The Capacity to Kill Oneself is Learned

Wanting to kill yourself is one thing. Actually being capable of it is another. Our instinctive will to live fights hard against the will to die, making it very difficult to follow through with a suicide, no matter how much pain, suffering, or psychache brings it on. People who are contemplating suicide often engage in counterintuitive behaviors. Carefully mending a severe but accidental cut or life-threatening wound, for example, suffered while rock-climbing or working on a house: if a person really wants to die, why not just use this as a means to that end and simply bleed out? The answer is that the will to live is consistent with our biology, and the desire to die is not. Some individuals have survived an attempt that should have killed them, like jumping off the Golden Gate bridge[19] or swallowing a bottle of sleeping pills. Many of these people report that in the moment between initiating the attempt and blacking out, they think in horror, *What have I done*? This ambivalence, this sense of noncommittal to suicide even as the attempt to die is underway, is further evidence of how wrong and how irrational suicide seems to the human mind.

To successfully complete a suicide, a person has to learn how to shut off the biological impulse to live and stay connected with other people. It's an insidious habituation to the awful things in life that make those things overtake the positive reasons for staying alive. This is part of why it's such a serious issue for veterans, who have seen more potentially traumatic sights during one tour of duty than the average civilian sees in a lifetime. Dr. Thomas Joiner, a leading researcher in the field of suicidology, has noted that the capacity to kill oneself takes fearlessness, not cowardice[20]. One needs to practice, become habituated to fear and pain through repeated suicide attempts or exposure to potentially lethal situations. A person needs to have little fear of death or pain, and that's exactly what veterans are trained to develop. Hence, the same training and experience that supply veterans with the courage to take a hill can mean that they're also unafraid of dying by their own hand.

RECONNECTING

There is some good news. The relationship between combat-related trauma and suicide is complex, and not every traumatized veteran will consider or attempt killing themselves. In fact, traumatic experiences in war can decrease one's risk for suicide by promoting positive feelings like being part of something larger than oneself, and a sense of being able to overcome what at first seem to be insurmountable obstacles. These experiences are not uncommon. And when processed normally and not sideswiped by the psychological effects of trauma, they help people develop into stronger human beings.

Among the up to 15% of veterans who do consider suicide, the truth needs to come out.[21] The causes of their suffering—post-traumatic stress and unresolved traumatic grief—are treatable. Moreover, their desire to kill themselves is not due to their own weakness, fallibility or a personal or genetic defect. It's rather the predictable consequence of trauma's effect on intelligent, competent, caring veterans. It can happen soon after leaving the warzone, or years, or decades, down the road. And the information needed to prevent suicides does not currently come from the government's many suicide-prevention campaigns; in fact, these campaigns contain some mistaken conclusions about the cause of suicide among traumatized veterans that can literally prove deadly.

BLAMING THE VICTIM

Psychologically speaking, military units can be thought of as a large, extended family, and the increasing number of suicides among service members a manifestation of a broader, system- or "family-"wide dysfunction. A parallel between traumatized veterans and family dysfunction/problem-resolution does indeed exist, and can be helpful to understanding the relationship between the military leadership and the service members who carry out its mission.

Frequently, individuals come to their first family therapy session having already identified one family member (often one of the children) as the root of that family's difficulties. *If only Jason would stop getting into trouble at school, our family would be fine.* One of the first goals of a family therapist is to help each family member realize that the person they want to blame for all their troubles may be the family's most compassionate member, suffering silently on the others' behalf. The tendencies of this person—the "black sheep" or scapegoat—to annoy or disrupt the family's harmony are actually frustrated expressions of this suffering and compassion. The blamed family member may be willing to suffer even to the point of feeling suicidal, thinking it crucial to protect the family from accepting any responsibility for their own dysfunction at all costs.

In 2010, the Pentagon, in an official report on the cause of the increased number of suicides among active-duty personnel, identified a number of issues, including relaxed standards for enlistment, lack of follow-up on expediently separating "high-risk" (potentially suicidal) service members, and taking steps to encourage high-risk service members to accept the treatment and help they need. The same report explicitly rejects the idea that multiple deployments—and the associated exposure to trauma—may be responsible for the increased suicide rate of active-duty service members[22]. This and similar reports suggest that the military and other government agencies bear no responsibility for the actions of certain high-risk individuals, instead shifting the blame by labeling these individuals as "too unhealthy" to deal with the stress of military service; that is, these reports imply that veterans and other traumatized service members who consider suicide should see themselves as defective, or at least lacking the resilience to deal with the stresses other "healthier" people can easily manage.

These messages, however explicit or subtle, can be deadly. Study after study has shown the number-one cause of suicide among Vietnam veterans is combat-related *guilt*: veterans kill themselves out of excessively compassionate responsibility for actions other members of their "family" (politicians, leaders, and Americans for whom these veterans have fought) collectively refuse to acknowledge or accept.

Part II

The GROWTH Model – Competency Based Recovery

CHAPTER 9

Natural Debriefing – An Introduction to the GROWTH Model

After World War II, hundreds of thousands of American soldiers returned to the U.S. by ship, telling innumerable war stories to each other during the voyage home. These WWII veterans weren't instructed as to what, how, or with whom they should share their stories about strife, loss, or victory in combat; they simply took the opportunity to express themselves among a fellowship of military brethren.

The experience of sharing stories after trauma and seeking community bonds isn't unique to war. Following the 9/11 attacks on the Twin Towers, more than 90% of Manhattanites sought out someone to talk with about what they saw, heard, and felt. When a child is killed in an accident, or at the hands of a criminal, parents, siblings, relatives, and friends are left devastated. But, while still in the throes of grief, they may organize a memorial service for the victim, coming together to collectively mourn their loss. When somebody has a close brush with death, surviving a nearly fatal car collision, for example, that person usually reaches out to a trusted friend to share feelings, fears, and memories of what happened.

These cases and countless others make something very plain: When people experience an unexpected tragedy, the spontaneous human response is to gather in a collective effort to recover, psychologically and emotionally. In nations and cultures worldwide, people demonstrate the human instinct to recover from a tragic event through a process called "natural debriefing[23]," in which individuals talk to others about unexpected, profoundly unfair, traumatizing events.

Veterans are familiar with debriefings. After-Action Debriefings recount the facts of a mission so that military leaders can evaluate what went "right" or "wrong." The purpose of natural debriefings is not so much to determine the "facts," but rather to encourage individuals to express subjective reactions to tragic, traumatic events—to get it off their chests, so to speak. Curiously, as the length of combat veterans' deployment increases, so does the length of their after-action debriefings; that is, they start to tell longer, more detailed, more subjective stories the longer they've been deployed. Not only do these veterans tell the basic facts of the mission, they also give details from their own, personal perspective. Subjective comments like *Did you see that!* and *I could not believe...* may not be considered mission-critical intel (intelligence), but they are part of how veterans naturally try to come to grips with memories of trauma.

This urge to express thoughts and feelings through natural debriefing is healthy, so long as the debriefings themselves are done under the proper conditions. But for many veterans it can feel foreign, debasing, or irrational. Many assume that PTSD-related symptoms are a problem for them and them alone, that they have to fix this problem on their own, and any expressions of strong emotion compromise and humiliate them. Moreover, if veterans try to talk about their experiences, especially to a civilian with no direct experience of combat, they can easily feel as if they're under the microscope of judgment, or feel that the listener is disgusted or disturbed by what they're hearing. This just leaves a veteran feeling more alienated than before.

How to Engage Veterans in Natural Debriefing

I lead my Traumatic Stress Recovery workshops with this mantra: *We're traumatized as individuals. We heal as a community.* The force of this statement underlies the essential role that veteran helpers—families, coworkers, therapists, and friends—play in helping veterans with PTSD-like symptoms. This section of this book introduces a six-step program that will help you assist veterans on the road to natural recovery. Before we start, there are some ground rules.

First, **help veterans you know**. For all of the reasons we've been examining throughout this book, veterans first and foremost, need to talk to someone they can trust, and that starts with the people closest to them. Don't try to reach out to just any veteran you may meet and offer to solve his or her problems; this approach will in all likelihood lead in the wrong direction.

Second, **always be honest**. A good listener has an extraordinary power to help people say things they need to say, even though they may feel ashamed, guilty, or troubled by expressing traumatic memories to another person. In some ways, it's like caring for a very sick person you know and love; you're not a doctor or a nurse, but you want to help—even though you know things could get uncomfortable, messy, and hard to handle. There are limits, however, for laypersons that play the role of caretaker or listener. If at any time, you feel unsafe or out of control, let the veteran know. Just like the veteran, you can stop at any time. It's unhealthy and counterproductive for a listener to feel out of control, and this feeling can come on quickly. If you feel like you can't keep listening, be honest and call for a time-out.

Third, unless you're asked directly to intervene, **don't try to offer advice or solve the veteran's problems.** While a veteran is telling stories of past trauma and how it's affecting them now, you may feel compelled to "do" something more than listen. It's only natural to want to help "fix" things, especially for someone you care about, and the urge to lend advice as well as a hand can be very strong. This can lead listeners to interrupt a veteran midstream with something like: *I know what you can do;* or *okay, but did you try...;* or *if only you'd do this...* Your intentions are good, but this approach doesn't help. The goal is for the veteran to get his or her story out in the open so that the veteran activates an emotion-based, traumatic memory in a safe versus traumatic context. Resist the urge to interrupt with advice; it's like damming or diverting the flow of the debriefing, and that does more harm than good.

Fourth, ***be aware of "logical" vs. "emotional" reasoning.*** Veterans continue to be bothered by past traumatic events because the experience destroyed basic core beliefs, and the restoration of these beliefs requires action as well as thought. Veterans may want to tell the same story (or portions of it) over and over again. This is normal and therapeutic; the process helps the brain recover the basic beliefs that trauma destroyed. It does no good to argue with a veteran or insist that they're not being rational. The unraveling of their problems takes place in the limbic, emotional center of the brain, and it's in the simple act of listening that you help a veteran straighten this tangle of problems out. Remember, talking about trauma takes time, emotional dedication, and patience.

Fifth, **listen actively**. This means giving the veteran 100% of your attention, and using your emotions as well as your mind to interpret what you're being told. We're all modern multi-taskers, and this happens when we listen, too. But with respect to traumatized veterans, you're not effective as a listener when you're watching TV, washing the dishes, or surfing the Net. Meeting face to face is best, because it allows you to take in the speaker's posture, expressions, and gestures as part of the communication. Talking on the phone means we miss all of these key non-verbal cues. It's also important to pick up on feelings hidden in the words a veteran speaks. You can practice this by listening and looking for verbal and non-verbal expressions of guilt, hostility, anger, frailty, shame, or fear.

Sixth, **give yourself sufficient time to listen and to respond**. Listening takes time, so you need to make sure you have sufficient time to give. You also need to place limits on the length of time in order to listen effectively. Professional therapists find that a great deal can be accomplished in 50-minute sessions. Clinical experience has shown that this gives patients sufficient time to open up about a difficult subject; at the same time, the 50-minute limit minimizes the risk of feeling emotionally overwhelmed during the session. Professional therapists train for years to be able to help individuals talk about difficult topics. If things get overwhelming for you, scale your listening time back by ten, twenty, or thirty minutes. If the veteran is really opening up, and you're still feeling capable of listening, don't feel the need to cut them off—go ahead and extend the time to let them continue to talk.

If you do begin to feel in over your head, or just saturated to the point of drowning in negative emotions yourself, take a break. Most importantly, make sure to tell the veteran you're helping that you feel this way, and that it's your strong feeling that it's time they speak with someone else and/or see a professional to continue the process of building themselves back up.

CHAPTER 10

GROWTH STEP #1 - GO TO A SAFE PLACE

In the military, one is taught to first break down problems into their component parts. Next, systematically assess risk and benefits, and alternatives to action. Finally, one determinates a course of action with explicitly defined end points. Frequently, service members (and veterans) express frustration with PTSD treatments, because the goals or "end points" of these treatments are not always explicitly defined. The GROWTH recovery model for veterans addresses this concern by having each of its six steps describe a specific, concrete action. The six steps of the GROWTH model are as follows:

G	**GO** to a safe place
R	**Relax**
O	**Open Up** to experience
W	**Wait** until you are ready
T	**Tell** your story
H	**Heal**

Each of these steps describes a *skill*, and like any set of skills, GROWTH will take time and effort to learn and apply. Here, and in the following chapters, we'll examine GROWTH steps one through six, looking not only at what veterans can do through GROWTH, but also what they can expect in terms of challenges and rewards.

Let's start with the first skill: ***Go to a safe place.***

Feeling Safe

Feeling physically and psychologically safe is an essential skill, and it's one that traumatized veterans need to relearn. Most of us take a general feeling of safety for granted—it's one of those basic beliefs that gets wrecked by trauma. Without the basic belief in safety, things like driving a car or going up in a skyscraper can become terrifying—a person thinks he'll be killed in a fiery collision or that terrorists might bomb the building. While people who haven't experienced trauma may acknowledge the distant possibility of such threats, they don't feel anxious about them all the time. To traumatized veterans, these kinds of threats can feel constantly imminent, putting them on guard at all times to defend against supposed threats to their safety.

A reliance on logical problem-solving, a faculty that serves us well in making good decisions in most aspects of life, actually makes things worse for traumatized veterans struggling to feel safe. This has to do with the biology of the brain and the changes brought about in it by trauma.

When something happens that alerts the brain to possible danger, the limbic brain reacts in about 12 milliseconds, causing us to startle and turn in the direction of the threat. It can take up to 30 milliseconds more for the human brain to follow up with what we discussed earlier as an "orienting response," where we try to become consciously aware of the source of the threat. Say you're sitting by a campfire at night and hear a twig break in the woods—the limbic brain springs into action and your head jolts to the side, unconsciously asking, "What was that?" Almost immediately afterwards, the conscious brain kicks in, processing any relevant data—any movement, any other strange sounds, any sensations you might pick up to tell you about the seriousness of the threat. If your human brain perceives a squirrel hopping from the direction of the sound, you calm down and turn back to the fire. If instead you hear a growl and see a grizzly bearing down on your campsite, the "fight or flight" response kicks in. This is how the body and brain are biologically engineered to deal with potential threats in a dangerous world, and 999 times out of a 1,000, the process works as it should to keep us safe.

Trauma messes with this engineering, because the abnormal memories created by trauma trigger sudden, strong negative emotions in the limbic brain. Instead of being activated only by threats that are perceived as imminent and real (the click of a gun's hammer, an explosive's crack and boom), the limbic brain reacts to benign stimuli; it could be the sight of a certain shade of blue, the scent of wax, the sound of a child whistling—none of which are dangerous or threatening in and of themselves, but in the context of a veteran's traumatic experience could be strongly associated with entrenched feelings of anger, stress, guilt, or fear.

When these benign stimuli appear, the veteran notices them, but is entirely unaware of *why* the limbic brain is shrieking into action—like the frantic crew of the sinking ship—in response to the threat. He or she responds to the signal of "threat" as triggered by the sight of a certain non-harmful person or color, or smell just as they would to a real threat—that is, the veteran startles, then tries to orient him or herself to the cause. The problem here is that there is no real threat, and thus no real cause that the human brain can perceive. This confuses the brain, creating feelings of stupidity (*Why can't I figure out what's going on?*), cowardice (*Why am I afraid of everything?*), or craziness (*Why am I so detached from reality?*). Since they can't react to a cause they can't perceive, instinct tells veterans to simply "get away." To get a sense of how this feels, imagine walking to your car in a deserted parking lot at night and being struck suddenly by a sense of dread—you don't know why you're scared, but impulse tells you to rush to your car, start it up, and get out of there ASAP. Traumatized veterans, too, want to get out of situations that are causing them to feel unsafe. But it's not as simple as just driving away, because the source of fear isn't in a parking lot, it's in their own heads.

This sense of dread can also ruin relationships with other people. When we're doing something with someone we like, most of us take it for granted that they won't try to hurt, confuse, insult, or endanger us for no reason. When studying for a test, for example, we assume our study partner is giving us correct, relevant information. But what if we lost this basic belief? What if all of a sudden we assumed that our study partner was misleading us, plotting to sabotage our performance on the upcoming test? Imagine that, against all logic, you were certain that this was true, that the study partner couldn't be trusted—what would you do? Stop studying with that person; in fact, get away entirely and study with someone you can trust.

HAVING FUN

So what can veterans do to regain trust in others and feel psychologically safe? The deceptively simple answer is "have fun." When we do something we enjoy, especially when that activity involves other people, we feel safe. Or put another way, if we didn't feel fundamentally safe when we were doing something, we wouldn't have fun doing it. This doesn't mean there isn't an element of danger or risk—you may feel psychologically on edge when matched against a master chess player, or physically threatened by the prospect of bungee jumping or playing a tackle football game. But if you still enjoy those activities, if you're having fun even while feeling an exhilarating fear, it means that you trust the people you're with. Conversely, if you think your chess opponent will cheat, that the bungee-cord operator will sabotage the line or that the football players will play maliciously to hurt you, there's no way you're going to have fun. Trust and feeling safe are key.

Hence, to regain a sense of safety and trust in others, veterans need to get out and do things they enjoy—with people they enjoy being with. For most PTSD-afflicted veterans, this isn't easy. The first step is to identify the places, activities, and people a veteran used to enjoy prior to his or her traumatic experience. If a veteran used to love to go fishing at Lake Luhr with his Uncle Joe, for example, but now just doesn't feel motivated, veteran helpers need to encourage him to grab his rod and head out—even if it seems like a waste of time and energy. In the same vein, if a veteran used to enjoy the movies, bowling, or target shooting with a certain person, veteran helpers need to get him or her back on the road to recovery by simply reintroducing the veteran to these enjoyable experiences. Remember: it's *experiences* that drive recovery, not the intellect; so even while faulty logic is saying there's no point to doing something, it is important to remember doing enjoyable activities actually creates the conditions, both biological and psychological, for natural recovery to occur. Here's how to begin.

First, come up with at least one activity that the veteran thoroughly enjoyed in the past. Next, find at least one person with whom the veteran has felt safe with—or can feel safe with—while doing this activity. For some veterans, this may be easy. Others may feel that there's no point, or that it's all just wishful thinking. If it seems impossible to identify a place, activity, and person or persons that a veteran can enjoy, find a competent individual—it could be a trusted family member, a member of the clergy, or a professional therapist—to intervene and help get the veteran on track.

Keeping Goals in Mind

Step One, Go to a Safe Place, lays the foundation for **GROWTH**. Feeling safe and doing fun activities with people you trust creates the conditions needed for natural recovery from trauma. But thinking about or talking about trauma is never fun or easy. For this reason, veterans need to identify a specific, tangible goal that has meaning for them. Just saying, "It would nice to get a better night's sleep," isn't enough motivation to move a person through the intense suffering that often accompanies the natural recovery process. Veterans who make the most of the **GROWTH** model are motivated by core goals like, "I want to be able to play with my grandchildren," "I don't want to get divorced," or "I don't want my kids to be messed up because I have PTSD."

It's been said that to endure any "what" one has to have a "why."[24] When service members deploy, they often take along a small reminder, like a picture or token of a loved one, to remind them of why they're fighting, why they're enduring terrible experiences, and why they need to return home safe. Veterans going through natural recovery need the same kind of motivation to remind them of why they're intentionally recalling and reliving experiences of trauma. Keep this in mind as we move through the subsequent steps of **GROWTH**.

CHAPTER 11

GROWTH Step #2: Relax

Most of us have had the experience of feeling so anxious that we couldn't relax—pacing the hospital halls waiting for a doctor's diagnosis, lying sleepless in anticipation of an upcoming job interview, or nervously waiting for a court's decision on some important matter. Hopefully, whether good or bad, a resolution comes, and the finality allows us to calm down, acknowledge our circumstances, and move on. In cases of anxiety disorders, however, feelings of intense anxiety get compounded, leaving the sufferer without recourse to relax.

PTSD falls into the category of anxiety disorders, and anxiety is at the heart of many PTSD-related problems. To recover the ability to relax, veterans need to learn how to dispel anxiety, on the level of both biology and behavior.

Relaxation, Part A: Turning off the Body's Anxiety Switches

As we've seen, the cycle of post-traumatic symptoms can be very hard to break, especially because veterans were never told that natural recovery is based on skills, not logic. Biological manifestations of anxiety—increased startle response, hyper-vigilance, difficulty keeping attention or focus—result from a hyperactive fight or flight response, the brain's lightning-quick warning system.

In the face of an unexpected threat, the fight or flight response prepares the body to physically do whatever's necessary to survive. Fight or flight is a function of the limbic brain; hence, it's not under our voluntary control, but activated automatically by sights, sounds, scents, tastes, or other sensations that seem threatening. When the response kicks in, the sympathetic nervous system acts like a gas pedal, revving up the body's RPMs: your heart rate rises, you take quicker breaths, your pupils dilate, and blood rushes to your brain, priming the body to attack, defend, or run away. Once the threat has passed, the parasympathetic nervous system acts like a break to decelerate the rush.

Deployed soldiers experience prolonged stretches of potentially life-threatening situations, and possibly traumatic events. As a result, their fight or flight instinct "overlearns" its response to a perceived threat and now acts as if the veteran is in an extremely dangerous, combat-like environment—back to the wall, eyes scanning the room, hands at the ready—even when he or she is perfectly safe[25]. Hence when veterans seem excessively "on guard," it's because the overactive limbic brain is telling their human brain that, at any moment, something bad is about to happen. Once activated, the sympathetic nervous system stomps on the gas, releasing an extra burst of energy that doesn't dissipate once the perceived threat has passed.

Veterans can't control this consciously; that is, they can't simply tell the limbic system to "cool off.[26]" But there is something they can do to reset the playing field. By repeatedly activating their parasympathetic system—the brake—they'll gradually undo the overlearned limbic behavior that's creating the mess of anxiety. One of the most effective ways of doing this is to teach yourself to breathe.

The art of taking breaths is central to many Eastern philosophies and spiritual traditions, whose practitioners believe that proper control of breathing is essential to reaching a state of enlightenment or peace. Most of the time, breathing comes naturally. We breathe deeply, quickly, slowly, or softly depending on the limbic system's response to stimuli. Controlled breathing overrides this system, bringing our breaths under our conscious control. Take a moment and breathe in slowly for a count of four. Now hold that breath for a count of four, then breathe out for a count of four. How do you feel? Chances are you are a measure more relaxed. The reason is that when we breathe slowly in and out, we're using our parasympathetic nervous system to slow down; taking the foot off the emotional gas, so to speak.

Doing this exercise once or twice makes you feel a little better for a few seconds, but it doesn't have a lasting effect. Doing it hundreds and hundreds of times, methodically, helps your nervous system adapt, making you more naturally, biologically equipped to handle anxiety. The goal is to practice this technique until the limbic brain unlearns the hyper-responsive reaction to perceived threats, and relearns its normal, useful, helpful biological response. This takes time, but the commitment pays off.

Veterans can also use progressive muscle relaxations, self-hypnosis, and other techniques to help undo the hyper-arousal effects of post-traumatic stress[27].

Relax, Part B: Staying in Control

One of our basic beliefs is that we can control our own thoughts, including being able to access memories when we want to, and turn them off when we don't. Flashbacks and other intrusive memories challenge this belief. Inexplicably, instead of being in the "here and now," veterans will suddenly see, smell, taste, feel, or hear something that happened months, years, or even decades before. This "memory" feels very present and very real, forcing a veteran to relive all or some of a prior traumatic event. Such an experience would make any person feel almost totally out of control, and in the case of flashbacks, measured breathing and other relaxation techniques won't have the same effect as on other sources of anxiety. But there's something else veterans can do to lessen their intensity.

Flashbacks, like all partially processed memories, are a function of the limbic brain, and shutting them down means getting the human brain back in control. Talking to yourself or trying to command your brain to relax in the course of a flashback is not only ineffective, it can actually make things worse. This is because your human brain controls the ability to talk to yourself—this ability doesn't involve the limbic brain, which can thus keep spending its energy on the flashback while the human brain wastes its energy trying to talk itself out of it. It's something like what would happen if a ship caught fire; the captain gets a call from the admiral, who asks how things are going:

CAPTAIN
Sir, I can't talk right now, the ship's going up in flames and I need to get it under control.
ADMIRAL
Captain, tell me in exact detail where the fire is spreading, how it started, and what you're doing to put it out.
CAPTAIN
Well, it's hard to describe, Sir, and like I said, I don't have the time with everything up in flames and the ship sinking into the sea.

What needs to happen instead is to get **the limbic brain focused on something else in its domain**—to drain *its* energy and exhaust the fire.

Another function of the limbic brain is to control bilateral, symmetrical behaviors, things like driving a car, walking, riding a bicycle, or playing the piano. The limbic brain has a finite amount of energy with which to carry out its functions. When the reserve gets low, the limbic brain stops working so hard, having less energy to devote to the intensity and "real-life" quality of a flashback. Hence, if you're having a flashback and start to walk, tap your fingers, move your eyes back and forth[28], or do any other activity involving symmetrical movement on both sides of the body, the limbic brain will divert energies to controlling this coordinated movement. Soon the flashback fades away. Once the human brain regains control, thinking about and talking about trauma in helpful, curative ways can resume.

CHAPTER 12

GROWTH Step #3: Open Up to Experience

When we talk about the "here and now," we mean the geese that we see passing over our heads, the ambulance siren we hear screeching through the streets a few blocks away, or the sight of a friend waving at us from across the train platform. We're not in the "here and now" when we ask, "I wonder where those birds are headed?" or "Was anybody hurt?" or "How long has it been since I've seen my friend?" The "here and now" is what we sense happening in the moment, as opposed to what we think about once the moment's gone.

This may seem obvious, but the distinction is important to veterans suffering from post-traumatic stress who often try to avoid the "here and now," steering away from situations or environments that may stir up intense feelings of anger, rage, fear, sadness, or helplessness. Veterans with chronic PTSD-type symptoms often report that despite their best efforts to control it, the brain seems to have a "life of its own", almost continually ruminating about past, negative events, or fixating on some possibly adverse event that might occur in the future. As with the psychological obstacles mentioned earlier, traumatized veterans see these concerns as rational based on what they know from prior experience. Remember that, unlike autobiographical, fully processed memories, the intensity of partially processed, trauma-induced memories heightens over time. Sights, sounds, images, and thoughts that had seemed merely unpleasant at the time become progressively more intense and disturbing, until even the idea of having to encounter these sensations is enough to motivate the human brain to do whatever it can to avoid them.

Fortunately, *it is possible to regain control.* Overly intense emotions have a weakness. All emotions, both positive and negative, need two elements in order to maintain their intensity—a human-brain element, which consists of thoughts, ideas and associations, and a limbic-brain element, which consists of various states of autonomic arousal and associated bodily sensations. If the intensity of either of these two elements is decreased, there is a corresponding decrease in the intensity of the emotion. Hence, a person can temper intense emotions by decreasing the intensity of bodily sensations or emotion-related thoughts[29], a therapeutic model that can work well for veterans with chronic PTSD-type symptoms.

In the short term, it can be very difficult to apply these techniques effectively when you're feeling very angry, sad, scared, or helpless. When you have an awful day at work and the boss blames it all on you, you might find yourself so furious you can't fall asleep. Thoughts and feelings associated with the day's events keep replaying themselves in your mind. At a certain point, you may realize that continuing to "think" about this problem is becoming counterproductive—no matter how hard you try, you can't justify or rationalize your boss's behavior or your own, and the intense feelings about the day don't subside. A proven method for turning down the intensity of these unhelpful, excessive emotions is to turn down the intensity of the bodily sensations associated with these emotions; once this takes effect, negative thoughts and feelings naturally decline. You feel better, more capable of living in the moment and in the world.

Tuning in to Your Senses: How to Focus on the Here and Now

By not experiencing "here and now" sensory input, veterans effectively become prisoners, trapped in their own heads, unable to experience positive and joyful aspects of their lives. Moreover, constantly "thinking" makes it impossible to finish processing trauma-induced memories, creating pitfalls that keep veterans from naturally recovering.

Imagine you're climbing a very steep, slippery slope of a hill. The rain's beating down, and every foothold and handhold you make requires every ounce of your concentration. Suddenly, inexplicably, your brain starts thinking about your next summer's vacation—what do you almost instantaneously do? Turn off these thoughts so that you can focus on moving your hands and feet in a coordinated, careful ascent to the top.

The brain has the ability to kick into this intensely focused mode to meet the challenges of intense situations, but veterans can use this to intentionally suppress thought during low-intensity, low-stress states as well. This happens when veterans focus their attention on "here and now" sensations. One way to do this is called the "grounding technique." Grounding goes by many names—mindfulness, mind-body bridging, centering, and creating a resting space. It is well known to practitioners of yoga and meditation. Our goal with this technique is to help veterans control the intensity of trauma-related, partially processed memories so that the limbic brain can naturally finish processing them.

To ground themselves, veterans need to learn how to tune out unwanted thoughts by tuning in to "here and now" sensations. Small children provide a perfect illustration for how this can be done. Small children are very sensory oriented. They love to touch, taste, smell, see, and hear new or interesting shapes, patterns, and textures. We lose some or all of this instinctual joy and excitement as we age, and our attention steers toward experiences that convey something logical, practical, and useful. An essential part of being grounded is rekindling a fascination and intrinsic joy in sensations. "Tuning in" to our senses means "tuning out" logical thought. Some people start by closing their eyes. Others find that tapping their finger or foot helps them focus. Practitioners of some forms of meditation turn off thoughts by focusing on nothing at all. In each case, a person lets thoughts pass through the mind without becoming hinged—the aim is to tune into *sensations*, not to get caught up in logical analysis or even reflective thought on what these sensations mean.

Let's turn again to controlled breathing to better understand how this works. Close your eyes and take in some deep breaths. Focus on the sensations associated with these breaths—the way the air feels, tastes, and smells; the rise and fall of your chest as you inhale and exhale; the sound of the air drawing in, then moving out. You might have some spontaneous thoughts in the process, like, *Why does my chest feel tight*? or *I need to vacuum*, or *That hickory smoke in the air is coming from the neighbor's barbeque.* When such thoughts come, simply acknowledge them and let them pass. This leaves the mind uncluttered, free and clear to observe and take joy in observation without being troubled with the heavy lifting of reflection or logical thought.

TURNING DOWN THE INTENSITY OF UNWANTED EMOTIONS

The grounding technique can help decrease the intensity of unwanted emotions as well as unwanted thoughts. The key, again, is to focus on specific sensations. We've seen how certain sensations can trigger unwanted emotions. When you shift focus from the "trigger" sensation to a "benign," "here and now" sensation, you disarm the unwanted emotion. These two steps done sequentially can be extremely effective in helping veterans control what at first feels like uncontrollable rage, sadness, or helplessness.

When we experience a feeling of intense sorrow, for example, we can often identify a place in our bodies where this feeling manifests itself as a physical sensation. You might feel tightness and dull pain behind your eyes; identify this as the location of the bodily sensation associated with the negative emotion (sorrow), *then turn your focus to another, unassociated sensation* (such as breathing). By turning attention away from the negative sensation, you're turning down the intensity of the sorrowful emotion.

As with the other steps of **GROWTH**, opening up to experience in the ways described above is a competency-based skill; one that builds, sequentially, on the previous skills taught in **GROWTH** steps one and two. Some veterans, based on their prior experiences and upbringing, will find grounding techniques and related skills intuitive and easy to learn. Other veterans will find them foreign, even frustrating to employ. The goal is to give them a shot; if they prove too difficult or simply don't have the desired effect after a few days or even weeks of practice, see a qualified therapist who can help guide you in ways specific to your situation.

CHAPTER 13

GROWTH Step #4: Wait Until You're Ready

Dealing with trauma-related issues is never easy. Even in the best of circumstances, the process of recovery taps into deep reserves of time, energy, and emotion, and these reserves can be hard to summon while you're dealing with other sources of intense stress in everyday life; in fact, doing so would make it impossible to function. The time to consider the moral, emotional and other implications of combat is not in the middle of a firefight. By the same token, attempting to delve into and resolve the intense emotions associated with a prior trauma won't work when you're so stressed out you're barely hanging on.

Moving through these GROWTH steps shouldn't feel like a race to the finish. PTSD-like symptoms can be so frustrating, depressing, or terrifying that veterans may want to put a rush on recovery, but one of the most important tenets of this method is to *wait until you're ready.* And being ready involves entering into an "optimal zone" for recovery.

The Optimal Zone for Recovery

In order to learn anything new, we need to find a middle ground between being bored or disinterested and the opposite—feeling hyper-anxious, terrified, or enraged. At either extreme, it's impossible learn or process new information. To finish processing (and fixing) trauma-induced memories, veterans need to find this optimal zone.

For veterans with PTSD-type symptoms, this zone comprises three variables of emotion, thought, and bodily sensation. The following table illustrates what it means to be "above," "below," or "within" the optimal zone of recovery.

Level of activation	**Level of Emotion**	**Thoughts**	**Bodily Symptoms**
Above optimal zone	**Excessive:** Feelings of extreme fear, panic, helplessness, rage, despair, shock, guilt, shame, or self-loathing	"Get me out of here!" "Help! I'm trapped!" "I can't think!" "It's never going to end!" "Things are out of control!"	Choking sensation Difficulty breathing Chest pain, severe nausea Dizziness, tingling around mouth, in fingers, pain in abdomen, severe headache
Within optimal zone	**Optimal:** Sadness, tearfulness, irritation, frustration, thoughtfulness, as well as some feelings of anxiety and/or nervousness	"I don't like how I'm feeling." "I know I'm going to be ok." "I'm feeling irritated" "I'm feeling sad" "I'm feeling concerned"	Wakeful, focused and aware of surroundings Somewhat faster rate of heart beats or breath Greater awareness of sights, sounds, scents Bodily sensations connected to trauma experience
Below optimal zone	**Insufficient:** Little or no emotional reaction to the topic, emotional numbness, mild irritation, sense of vague anxiety	"I'm bored" "This is a waste of time" "I would rather be doing almost anything else"	No symptoms, or mild nausea Sense of unease

The goal is for veterans to be able to use their own thoughts, emotions, and bodily sensations as guideposts to let them know if they're above or below the optimal zone—that is, whether now is the right time to start, or to continue, with a program that helps the limbic brain naturally recover from trauma.

It's common for veterans to try to make trauma-related problems go away when the veteran is still outside the optimal zone—when they're enraged, for example, or having a panic attack. But just like with the breathing techniques described earlier, it can be extremely difficult, if not impossible, to effectively put recovery techniques to use when symptoms are at their most intense. Some veterans, especially those who tend to "live in their head", may have a very difficult time identifying emotions associated with different "zones" of recovery. Others may find it one of the easier competencies to master. In either case, one of the most common reasons veterans find that they remain stuck, ***below*** their optimal zone for natural recovery, is due to symptoms of a related condition that is extremely common in deployed veterans: unresolved traumatic grief

Identifying Unresolved Traumatic Grief

Grief is a curious phenomenon. On the one hand, we need to experience grief to deal with unexpected loss, and nearly every human being on the planet experiences this need at some point in their lives. In this sense, grief is a shared, cross-cultural phenomenon, but on the other hand grief is a deeply personal, subjective experience defined and affected by each individual's personality, age, gender, culture, ethnicity, and religious or spiritual persuasions; hence, no two individuals grieve in exactly the same way. Given this objective/subjective axis of grief, it's almost impossible to prescribe or predict how a given active-duty service member or returning veteran should grieve traumatic, personal losses. Traumatic grief is similar to "simple" grief. But traumatic grief stems from a profoundly personal loss complicated by having occurred unexpectedly and in the context of a traumatic event. Moreover, as with all personal loss, traumatic losses need to be appropriately grieved. A failure to do so leads to predictable, and oftentimes extremely serious, long-term adverse effects.

Unresolved traumatic grief manifests as a collection of symptoms that may include feeling chronically inactive, emotionally detached, numb, and depressed. Veterans suffering from unresolved traumatic grief feel a sense of emptiness or hopelessness, unrealistic or irrational guilt, loneliness, excessive worry about their own and others' safety, intense or easily triggered anger or rage, and even utter worthlessness as human beings.

Traumatic grief occurs when veterans lose something very important to them, like a close friend or fellow service member, in an unexpected, catastrophic manner. One reason veterans are unable to resolve traumatic grief is that so many individuals and institutions confront them with the opposite of what are helpful statements that border on the accusatory, like "get over it," "suck it up," or "all this talk is for weaklings." These kinds of comments don't help veterans recover; they keep them stuck.

At the same time, it's clear that doing nothing, or not having the opportunity to grieve at all, is putting literally hundreds of thousands of combat veterans on a disastrous track. As we discussed in chapter eight, many will consider suicide and engage in excessive risk-taking behaviors. There are jails from coast to coast whose inmates include combat veterans; a history of their wartime experiences will turn up a very high rate of unresolved grief and loss.

Resolving traumatic grief is a deeply personal process, and you may question how, as a veteran helper, you can assist a veteran in addressing grief from the "outside in." The answer is to use a simple guideline to track a veteran's progress through personal experiences of grief: *If the quality of a veteran's personal and intimate relationships is the same, or better, than it would have been had a veteran not experienced this trauma, he or she is doing all right.*

In other words, the "acid test" for recovery from grief is based on how a veteran is functioning in the here and now of everyday life. If he or she seems emotionally connected to others, generally happy, or at least relatively content and satisfied with his or her life and daily affairs, they're effectively doing well. Remember that it's up to no one else but the veteran—given that the above holds true and he or she is functioning well—how much grieving a traumatic loss requires; hence, don't try to make a veteran who is functioning well grieve more just because you think he or she hasn't grieved enough, no matter how horrific the past story of trauma may seem to you. Conversely, if a veteran you know and love continues to be excessively irritable, angry, emotionally distant, and aloof, even though he or she claims to have already "dealt with" these prior traumatic events, the question of grief is clearly unresolved.

Getting to the Optimal Zone Through Ritual and Routine

What can a veteran or veteran helper in the latter case do to resolve grief and find the optimal zone to continue recovery? *The answer is to use rituals and routines to help create the conditions for natural recovery to occur.* Rituals are symbolic of something larger than the actual actions and items being used to perform them. For example, when we raise an American flag, we're raising more than a piece of colored, patterned cloth; we're declaring our allegiance to the United States, its principles and history, its citizens, and its service men and women. Every one of us has routines, and though routines lack the pomp and circumstance of ritual, they are immensely important to who we are and how we function in the world. Simple routines like brushing our teeth, taking the kids to school and picking them up, watching Monday Night Football with friends at the house, or running three miles every morning are not mere chores; they keep us healthy and strong, they show love and respect for ourselves and others, and they demonstrate the will to create the conditions necessary to heal, or simply to have a good time. Rituals and routines keep the limbic brain active and connected in constructive ways for recovery. Doing something like visiting the Vietnam Memorial in D.C. is an example of a ritual; there may be no logical purpose in it, and a traumatized Vietnam veteran may not see a point in the exercise, but it provides for an experience that can immensely help the brain fully process traumatic memories, grief, and loss[30].

CHAPTER 14

GROWTH Step #5: Tell Your Story

Progress through the first four steps of GROWTH prepares veterans for a very active stage in the recovery process: natural debriefing, or telling a personal, experiential story. The step described in the last chapter—Wait Until You are Ready—is very important. Only when veterans have entered the optimal zone for recovery should they try to tell their story about their traumatic experience[31]; otherwise, it could be too upsetting, overwhelming, and actually detrimental to healing. But when veterans are ready, when they've found that optimal zone, storytelling becomes a crucial part of the healing process.

You may have heard the phrase "a story is all in the telling." In other words, the power of a story, its emotional impact, has to do not only with the factual details, but with the teller's connection to them—the truths, if you will, that the teller can dig deep enough to find in the story and the courage to reveal these truths. The same holds true for telling stories of trauma. The intent of **GROWTH Step Number Five** is to facilitate the processing of trauma-induced, emotion-based, partially processed memories. Telling your story helps the limbic brain do this by translating chaotic, disorganized accounts into integrated, linear stories. It also creates a means for a shared, interpersonal experience of intense, trauma-related memories, something that is often a precondition for fully processing these memories.

Filling in the Missing Pieces

Once of the diagnostic criteria for PTSD is an inability to remember important aspects of the traumatic event. Some veterans don't report this as a problem; they remember what happened all too well. For others, however, intrusive recollections and flashback-type experiences are all the more disturbing because they're "out of the blue", and they don't make sense. Instead of flashing back to a specific time or place, veterans experience a collage of unrelated sights, sounds, smells, tastes, and sensations. It's like their brain is reproducing a very complex, multi-dimensional jigsaw puzzle of people, places, and events in time, and the puzzle's missing several key pieces. Before the limbic brain can make sense of these memories and integrate them with the rest of a veteran's long-term, autobiographical memories, it needs additional raw data (i.e., data from the primary senses) to finish the basic, crude picture.

The human, rational brain can help the limbic brain by consciously identifying as many sights, sounds, smells, tastes, and sensations that the veteran perceived at the time of the trauma, giving the limbic brain more data with which to work. When it comes to identifying, processing, and organizing disparate elements of a story, the human brain consciously gathers data that's fed into the "computer" of the limbic brain. The human brain has only an opaque knowledge of how the "computer" is working to process this data; it just has to trust that the limbic brain is in fact working out all the details and delivering them as a coherent story so the veteran can grasp and understand. In this way, the human brain assists the limbic brain in fixing traumatic memories, and storytelling is at the center of how the human brain gathers the necessary data.

TELLING AN EXPERIENTIAL STORY

For the limbic brain to create a coherent, linear account of trauma, veterans need to learn to tell an "experiential story." An experiential story is one where the listener feels like he or she is experiencing the events described in a tangible, even realistic way. Rather than just focusing on the facts, any good storyteller will describe each scene replete with sights, sounds, tastes, scents, and other sensations and actions that rattle or soothe the senses. Movie directors and master storytellers will say: "We have to *feel* it," and they mean this literally. Facts are objective; they keep the story suspended above the emotional waters, but facts alone don't create a memory that's rich enough to be processed by the human brain. The merely factual, objective storyteller's trauma therefore remains unresolved.

Compare the following two stories about a novice snowboarding experience:

> I took I-70 up to Keystone on March 1, 2011, to snowboard with my brother Jeff. The fresh snowpack was at 18 inches; temperature was 35 degrees. There were about 100 to 200 individuals in head-to-toe winter gear on the slopes. I tripped when I tried to get onto the ski lift with

> my Burton snowboard and oversized boots; I stumbled when I tried to get off. By the end of the day I'd had perhaps two successful runs. We stayed in a 10' by 15' room, without a private bathroom, at the lodge and left the next day for home.

This account is coherent, linear, and somewhat detailed when it comes to the facts, but the *experience* is sorely missing. Here's another, more experiential description of events:

> I caught a distinct chill as we passed through the darkness of the Eisenhower Tunnel on our way up to Keystone in early March. The chill, in part, was from the still-wintry air shivering through the high valley, but also from the echoing, mechanical rush of cars through the tunnel, and from the stillness and crisp winter glare of the sun when we passed through to the other side. The twists and turns of the mountain roads—winding and winding, upward and down—made my stomach slosh and the gall rise in my throat. But soon we were at the resort and when I got out of the car, leaned against the door, closed my eyes, and tilted my face toward the sky, the sun's warmth put my whole body at ease. My boots eased down into the soft, freshly fallen snow. My brother Jeff and I were there to snowboard, and a couple hundred other slope-runners rushed past us on either side, either as a "whoosh" at the end of a run down the mountain, or with a nudge or brush against our downy winter coats. The scent of the aspen groves came like an earthy perfume on the light breeze, mixed with the oily scent of

> diesel as the ski lift's engine chugged, clanged, and churned nearby.

This could go on, describing not only the strict floor plan of the room in which the friends stayed, but the efforts not to bump into each other in the dark, the texture of the cot in one corner, and the uncomfortable trek to the bathroom across the icy planks of the exterior corridor in the middle of the night.

The effect of the second story, and its distinction from the first, is clear. Only the second gives the reader a tangible, palpable sense of the excitement, trepidation, and wonder of the experience. When telling a story connected to a traumatic event, only the experiential version provides the limbic brain with the sensory data it needs to fill in the gaps of an only partially processed, trauma-induced memory.

Two are Better Than One

Traumatic events are so painful and emotionally distressing that the sufferer may not have the capacity to deal with them on his or her own. This is one of the primary roles of a therapist, who provides an "emotional vessel" into which individuals can pour angst and emotions that otherwise have no outlet. The need for other people to help us deal with intensely upsetting emotions is not just psychological. There is well established evidence proving that telling experiential stories to an outside listener can increase the biologic capacity of our brains, helping us deal with potentially overwhelming emotions.[32] Take for example, the act of comforting a crying baby. We do this intuitively, because we know that babies have a very rough time trying to calm themselves down on their own; they need the comforting touches, sights, scents, and sounds of another caring human being.

This need continues into adulthood, but it takes on different, more appropriate forms that coincide with a person's growth and development. It's analogous to watering newly planted seedlings in a garden. Initially, it's important to supply only sparse amounts of water. If you were to blast the plants with a hose, they'd wash away before they had a chance to take root. Once the plant has established roots and stalk, however, and is standing firmly on its own, its need for water—and the amount of dousing it can withstand from say a storm—increases dramatically.

Parents act as "water-flow regulators" to dampen the intensity of, for lack of a better term, life experiences for their young children. When the flow of stress starts to get too heavy, parents and other caring individuals turn down the tap to a manageable, safe level. As children mature into adulthood, they're assumed to have a much higher tolerance for stress; however, some situations are so inherently, intensely stressful that even mature, well developed, emotionally secure adults cannot process them without outside help. This certainly applies to veterans, who are extraordinarily likely to encounter traumatic events in the course of their military and subsequent lives. They need someone to act as an emotional regulator to help them decrease the emotional intensity brought on by memories of trauma. As long as a parent or caregiver is consistently there to soothe a child's tantrum, the child's brain and emotions develop along normal lines. When such a figure is absent from the child's life, the risk of developing long-term psychological problems is severe[33].

As with the other steps in GROWTH, "telling your story" is triage-based. Triage is a medical term that refers to the process of classifying patients based on degree of medical severity; or, as in this case, response to treatment. If a veteran is able to stay within their optimal zone for recovery, talking about prior trauma can be very therapeutic, allowing the primitive brain to convert trauma-induced, emotion-based memories into "human" brain, logic-based memories. If, however, attempts to "Tell Your Story" only result in additional suffering without any obvious, tangible benefit, a veteran should be "triaged" to a higher level of care. In practice, nine times out of ten, this means referring this veteran to a mental health professional.

CHAPTER 15

GROWTH Step #6: Heal

Recovery from the psychological effects of trauma is a process, not a product. The trajectory of recovery varies from veteran to veteran, and so do the outcomes. Veterans will still experience some suffering, or continue to be bothered by prior traumatic events. Recovery is *defined not by the absence of suffering, but by the presence of healing.* Through healing, the suffering associated with unexpected, painful recollections of a prior trauma will decrease to the point that it no longer stands in the way of a veteran's pursuit of a happy, fulfilling life.

You've heard of "healing waters," and we can think of healing as a continual flow. Traumatic experiences and memories build up a boulder of hard sediment that blocks and diverts the river's course, but over time the waters flow over and break down that boulder. The river courses on, stronger and swifter than before. Veterans heal by breaking down the two most debilitating effects of trauma: excessive activation of the fight or flight response, and the trauma-induced beliefs that make it so hard to move on.

Reversing the Biological Symptoms of PTSD

The core biological problem associated with PTSD is the excessive triggering of the fight or flight response, a consequence, as we discussed earlier, of overlearned behavior. GROWTH Step Number Two (Relax) shows how to reverse this hyperactive tendency by repeatedly activating, and then relaxing, the body's fight or flight response in reaction to *non-traumatic* triggers. GROWTH Step Number Six extends this approach to traumatic cues.

To accomplish this, a veteran needs to pair the "systematic desensitization" technique shown earlier with the other competencies of GROWTH, including being able to stay in control under stress, turning off thoughts and tuning in to experience, and continuing only while still in the optimal zone for recovery. Furthermore, to minimize the risk of becoming traumatized again, veterans should master using this technique in a controlled, safe environment (in vitro exposure) before putting it to use in a real-world situation (in vivo exposure).

In vitro exposure relies on the power of imagination. A veteran who was traumatized when an IED blew up his Humvee may have a strong, sudden, adverse reaction to the scent of diesel fuel. To undo the potency of this reaction, the veteran should begin by imagining the scent of diesel fuel, letting the mind, so to speak, breathe it in. The veteran could also look at a picture of their own or a similar Humvee, or hold an empty fuel can to help them conjure up the scent. Once the veteran is able to successfully expose himself to this imagined stimulus without an excessive, negative reaction, he may be ready to move on to in vivo exposure—that is, to the actual stimulus itself. In the hypothetical case above, this could mean actually sitting in a similar vehicle or filling up with a similar smelling fuel.

This build up to and through in vivo, real-world exposure is part of what we call "hardiness," a vital part of the healing process. When veterans become hardy enough to block out or withstand the biological responses to traumatic triggers. they can endure, and moreover enjoy, aspects of life from which trauma had made them shrink away.

Fixing Trauma-Induced Faulty Beliefs

Trauma can cause veterans to lose faith in themselves, others, and the world around them. As we've seen, these changes in belief are all the more destructive, because veterans assume that they're founded on logic; that is, the absence of trust comes as a logical consequence of the unexpected, horrifying, shocking experiences that traumatized veterans endure in war. Such sweeping generalizations, however, are neither practical nor logical. It's just that when basic beliefs are destroyed in the limbic brain, the human brain interprets this as having a logical basis; it's saying, in effect, that "there must be a good reason for this." The flip side of this is that because these beliefs are not in fact logical, logic and reason can't fix them. Hence, as veteran helpers, we don't want to logically "convince" veterans not to have faulty beliefs; this is an ineffective approach, almost like arguing in an alien language. Veterans may feel justifiably cynical or skeptical about specific groups, organizations, and individuals as a result of what they experienced in the field of combat. The goal is to help a veteran's limbic brain regain pre-trauma, *experience-based* beliefs about the world.

The best way to address trauma-induced faulty beliefs is by comparing a veteran's pre- and post-trauma attitudes and behaviors. With basic beliefs intact, people (including veterans) act in specific and characteristic ways. They take care of themselves, they avoid self-destructive behaviors, they do things that create and maintain emotional connections with others, and they actively pursue new accomplishments at work and home.

Veterans whose basic beliefs have been destroyed act in the reverse. They're frequently self-destructive, emotionally listless or irritable, and lack passion, focus, and serious life goals. As noted in earlier chapters, the transformations veterans go through from pre- to post-deployment can range from subtle to profound. There are simple questions to ask and tendencies to observe to help gauge the degree of negative change. Does a veteran you know and love respond freely to questions and engage in conversation, or is he or she distant, elusive, or scornful? Does he or she participate in family gatherings (even a simple evening meal), or does he or she uncharacteristically retreat from these kinds of rituals and routines? In the case when a traumatized veteran has gone seriously downhill in terms of happiness, passion for life, concern for him or herself and others, and enjoyment of activities and people he or she used to love, you can be fairly certain that trauma has deteriorated the veteran's basic beliefs.

So what can be done? Fixing trauma-induced beliefs requires that veterans have new experiences that support the basic beliefs they held prior to trauma. One method of achieving this is called the OIA technique—***Observe, Imagine, Act.***

The "**observe**" element is what we described above, namely paying attention to differences in a traumatized veterans behavior vs. how they behaved prior to trauma. It's important to stress that *veterans can observe themselves*—albeit to greater or lesser extents. In doing so, veterans should try to observe how their actions on a day-to-day basis differ from how they would have acted before they were deployed. As a veteran helper, the more specific you can be in these observations, the better; "You haven't met with us for our regular Sunday meal in two months" is more helpful than "You seem distant."

Imagination is key to regaining basic beliefs. Traumatized veterans should imagine, in the best possible scenario, acting in ways they used to act pre-deployment. "The best possible scenario" is an important distinction; many veterans will say that they could try to be more friendly, more involved, more eager to pursue things that make them happy, but that the effort would be utterly futile. This is the limbic brain trying to decide what's in the veteran's best interests, and as we've seen, rationalizing isn't an effective way of rebuilding basic beliefs. Imagining the best possible scenario, no matter how fantastical or impossible it may seem, helps veterans break through this "logical/illogical" barrier to trust in basic beliefs.

Action follows observation and imagination. Action is the final, crucial strep that allows recovery to occur. To heal, traumatized veterans need to act in ways consistent with their pre-trauma beliefs. At the same time, it's important to take things slowly. Basic beliefs are the creation of innumerable experiences, some immense, some barely a blip on the radar, from our childhood. Regaining these beliefs is a process that requires the accumulation of many positive experiences, and this can take a lot of patience. Say you're an expert surfer, and so is your friend. One morning in the waves outside Perth, your friend is struck and mauled by a Great White shark. Her physical wounds heal, but her emotional wounds will take more time. The attack was a freak occurrence. A shock. A once-in-a-lifetime phenomenon. But of course, it doesn't feel that way to your friend. She feels as if the threat is biting at her toes the instant they're washed with the froth of the waves. At first she withdraws, but with the encouragement of many, many successful, safe attempts at getting closer to the beach, the water, its increasing depths and its cresting waves, she has the chance of pursuing the experience of surfing again. Something she had always loved doing becomes something she loves to do again. For traumatized veterans, the same hope exists.

Part III

Additional Actions to Help Veterans

CHAPTER 16

Re-Evaluate the Notion of a "Cure"

On May 9th, 2009, Dr. Sanjay Gupta, a well-known medical personality on cable news, was asked the following question on the CNN American Morning show: "Do PTSD symptoms ever go away?" Dr. Gupta answered, "No." He said that the severity of symptoms can wax and wane, but PTSD is something one has "for life." He's not alone in his assertion. Government and non-government experts and agencies strongly imply the same thing through statements, articles, and materials on PTSD. The message is: when you've got PTSD, you've got it for good.

Think about the effect of such an assertion. Suppose you found out you might have an incurable disease, one that would seriously compromise your future prospects and create an unconquerable uphill battle lasting your entire life. Would you seek out an official diagnosis to know "for certain," or would you steer clear of the physician, preferring instead not to receive such devastating news? And then there's the subject of treatment—if you are ill, but don't understand your illness and don't want to know more out of fear, how do you make any progress to improve your health? Veterans deserve help, and the message that PTSD cannot be effectively treated does them a disservice, making it more likely that veterans will continue to actively avoid treatment. Moreover, this message is absolutely untrue. PTSD does not have to be a permanent condition. To understand how effective treatment can be, we have to re-examine what we mean by "cure."

Symptom Reduction

Recovery from a disease is judged according to how far you've returned to the state before you got sick; that is, you've recovered to the extent that you're no longer experiencing symptoms of an illness. What defines a medical cure, however, has to do with etiology, or the cause, of an illness. Eliminate the cause and you're cured. So let's say you have an infection; the doctor prescribes an antibiotic, the bacteria causing the infection are destroyed, and you've been cured.

Psychological disorders are different in that, generally, the "cause" for them is unknown. That is, a doctor can't isolate something like bacteria or a broken bone that, when "fixed," will cure the patient of his or her sickness. Hence, a "cure" for a psychological disorder has to do with how far a patient has recovered. When he or she no longer meets the diagnostic criteria for a disorder like social phobia or PTSD, we say they've been cured.

In large epidemiological studies, approximately one-third of the individuals studied continued to have PTSD symptoms after a period of five years; furthermore, it was projected that some individuals suffering from PTSD would continue to have symptoms for many years, possibly even decades. It should be noted that the risk for chronic symptoms is much higher in combat veterans as compared to their civilian counterparts.

But PTSD is treatable, and in multiple ways. The same studies noted above showed that two-thirds of individuals diagnosed with PTSD—a large majority—no longer met the diagnostic criteria for PTSD within a period of five years[34]. Clinical treatments, such as prolonged exposure therapy and cognitive processing therapy, have been shown in study after study to be effective for veterans with chronic PTSD. In fact, following an 8 to 12 week course of treatment, most veterans no longer meet the diagnostic criteria for PTSD[35].

Natural Recovery

If you're a veteran and have experienced a traumatic event, you're almost certain to develop at least some symptoms of PTSD. That's part of the reality of trauma, war, and the human psychological and biological disposition. Fortunately, for most veterans, these symptoms will gradually diminish and resolve over time through a process we can call "natural recovery[36]." It's important to emphasize that almost every veteran's life is upset to varying extents by the experience of trauma. As we saw in earlier chapters, trauma creates abnormal memories and shatters basic beliefs related to veterans' perception of themselves, others, and the world around them. Natural recovery occurs in response to these normal, predictable, trauma-induced biological and psychological effects. In other words, veterans can become able to biologically complete the process of processing these trauma-induced abnormal memories and psychologically regain the pre-trauma basic beliefs that defined how they thought of themselves and helped them accomplish things in the world.

Natural recovery is possible, but veterans can't afford to simply wait things out and let time heal. The ability to naturally recover depends, among other variables, on an individual's genetics, coping skills, and the extent of the trauma he or she experienced in war. But the most important variable has to do with what a veteran knows about PTSD. It's not that a veteran lacks the capacity to recover; it's that they were never taught how. This gives new context to a "cure" for PTSD. Given enough time, motivation, and practice, the majority of veterans can naturally recover.

The military uses training techniques to help soldiers overcome incapacities related to their potential to fight. Here's one example from my personal experience in the army: every soldier has to pass basic CTT or "Common Task-Training" skills evaluations. These skills include firing a weapon and donning a gas mask within certain tolerances for accuracy and time. When I joined the army, I had never fired a weapon. The first time I hit the range to fire my 9mm, the sergeant in charge commanded me to use my right hand, even though I'm left-handed. I tried my best, but failed to qualify. Here's the key point: the sergeant's response was not "Fohrman, you can't fire worth a damn. Turn in your weapon; you're done." Instead, it was to immediately send me to remedial training with the military police to get my shooting skills up to par. And this worked—I learned to shoot and qualified. I didn't give up, and the army didn't give up on me just because my initial attempt was unsuccessful. In fact, the assumption is that every recruit will learn the essential skills of a combat soldier. Failure is not an option.

The same approach needs to be taken in cases of veterans struggling to cope with PTSD. It's challenging to learn how to recover, but it's also essential. Some veterans learn these skills quickly. Others find the process more arduous, and in truth it can take some time. In no case is it impossible, however, so long as there are people there to encourage and guide the process.

Quality of Life

To enhance their quality of life, many veterans want to erase all memories of a traumatic event; that's their chief goal, to eliminate symptoms by eliminating traumatic memories that bring those symptoms about. It's an understandable rationale: forget the traumatic event ever happened and you'll go back to the way things used to be.

We can't, however, change the past, and we can't forcibly repress memories of it, at least not without damaging side-effects. And there's another reason why the denial or eradication of bad memories approach lacks force. Namely, it is because for many veterans, the very traumatic events that continue to haunt them may become one of the fundamental and defining experiences of their lives. Traumatic events are in another way like a serious illness. They're unfair. They cause intense suffering and pain. No one can avoid them with 100% certainty. But just as with an illness, we can take measures to improve our quality of life while progressing to whatever extent possible on a road to recovery. The question becomes: how can a veteran return to his or her previous quality of life—or even improve on it—following a traumatic event?

CHAPTER 17

Suffering, Courage and the Hero's Journey—The Path to Post-Traumatic Growth

The story of Britain's King Arthur is familiar worldwide. It's a legend not only of a heroic king, but of that king's struggle toward redemption. Arthur's campaign for the Holy Grail results in atrocities of battle, and the death and destruction of many of his fellow Knights of the Round Table. Arthur himself suffers subsequent betrayals from his wife (Guinevere), his most trusted knight (Lancelot), and even his son (Mordred). The whole of Camelot, a once glorious realm of fantastical beauty, wealth, and peace, begins to decay; and, in the midst of his suffering, Arthur himself draws away from his land and people. Yet from deep within himself, and with the help of friends like Bedevere, Perceval, and Merlin, Arthur rises back up, more than ever committed to his cause and his kingdom. He dies heroically, inspiring soldiers and chroniclers for eras to come.

Like all myths and legends, the story of King Arthur reflects universal human character traits and experiences, such as jealousy, anger, forgiveness, pride, tragedy, loss, and redemption. These stories also feature a hero who, following a downfall, manages to accomplish even greater, seemingly impossible, feats of strength and courage. In modern psychological parlance, we call this "post-traumatic growth."

Post-Traumatic Growth in Veterans

Post-traumatic growth refers to the experience of positive psychological development as a long-term consequence of an extremely adverse or traumatic situation. Philosophers, storytellers, and theologians have espoused the virtues of suffering for thousands of years in texts, myths, and biblical stories that draw upon tales of overcoming harsh trials and tribulations. Only recently have scientists put this under the lens of systematic study. In 1996, Drs. Tedeschi and Calhoun published evidence in support of their newly created "post-traumatic growth inventory.[37]" The authors developed the inventory as an instrument to "assess (for) positive outcomes reported by persons who have experienced traumatic events.[38]" These positive outcomes manifest in three ways: perceived changes in self-perception; a changed sense of one's relationships with others; and a changed philosophy or outlook on life.

Perceived change in self-perception refers to a post-trauma feeling of strength, self-assuredness, confidence, and the ability to deal with unexpected psychological or physical challenges. *A changed sense of one's relationships with others* involves feeling closer to friends and family, forging more meaningful relationships, and having an enhanced ability to meet emotional needs by accepting help and becoming more sensitive to the needs of other people. *A change in philosophy* means changing one's outlook and beliefs to better appreciate and participate in the experience of being alive; that is, you no longer take life for granted, but live each day to the fullest. This aspect of post-traumatic growth can also involve strengthening one's religious or spiritual beliefs.

Challenges to Post-Traumatic Growth

From the perspective of many veterans with PTSD-like symptoms, their traumatic experience yields absolutely no benefits; the unexpected, unfair, emotionally devastating events they experienced in war bring with them nothing redeeming, only continued horrors. But, it's from this kind of extraordinary experience that a person learns how to get stronger, how to deal with events of this kind—some of the worst that any human being is likely to face—with courage, compassion, intelligence, and valor, the hallmarks of a hero.

Take a moment to think of a time when you did something you are very proud of or learned what turned out to be an important "life lesson." Chances are you are thinking of an achievement or event that involved a lot of time and/or emotional effort. Being the fastest runner in your school is less of an accomplishment if you are naturally a very fast runner. The same accomplishment is much more meaningful if you had to overcome an injury or some other setback on your way to becoming the fastest runner.

The experience of post-traumatic growth depends on this aspect of extremely challenging circumstances, something that the average person, without an external source of motivation, is unlikely to ever experience. The people of Camelot did not, as a rule, appreciate the remarkable bounty of their king and realm, or believe that it could be fractured. King Arthur and many of his knights felt the stab of threats to the kingdom directly, and worked as a result, and sometimes to the point of self-sacrifice, to achieve peace and prosperity. If such threats and challenges never arose, there would have been no motivation to build such a remarkable kingdom, civil society, or legion of elite knights in the first place. Veterans suffer direct exposure to trauma, but this puts them in a similarly unique position to become stronger, more elite human beings as a result of their experience. Trauma works like a catalyst for this personal, physical, psychological, and spiritual growth to occur.

Natural Recovery: A Heroic Journey

Veterans have the capacity for decisive, lethal action when faced with danger. And as we saw earlier, this capacity is driven by compassion and care for their fellow service members and themselves. PTSD-type symptoms develop only when people who exhibit strength, sense of purpose, and compassion feel compelled to take on tasks that can result in what seems like an interminable, unbearable amount of suffering. There is a cross-cultural archetype associated with undertaking seemingly insurmountable challenges for the sake of others: the hero.

In *The Hero with a Thousand Faces,* Joseph Campbell explains that myths from across the centuries and the globe share a common narrative structure, one he terms the "monomyth." Dr. Campbell describes the monomythical hero thus:

> "A hero ventures forth from the world of common day into a region of supernatural wonder: fabulous forces are there encountered and a decisive victory is won: the hero comes back from this mysterious adventure with the power to bestow boons on his fellow man.[39]"

Often, the hero is reluctant to accept the call to duty, sometimes because he holds his own abilities in doubt. A reverend man or woman of the community, steeped in experience and wisdom, might help the hero learn essential skills or knowledge that will push him to persevere and overcome the challenges ahead. Next, comes a series of trials, some of which the hero survives on his own, others with the help of compatriots. The most intense part of the narrative involves the most severe challenges, where the reward for the hero's survival is a great gift or "boon"—a fabulous object, lands, kingship, or a legacy that will outlive the hero's own years. The hero must now decide whether to return to the ordinary world—a journey homeward that can be as perilous as the journey out. If the hero returns successfully, he will be able to share the boon with the world. As a result of his harrowing adventures, the hero becomes a master of two realms, able to deal with the practical problems of the "everyday" as well as the extraordinary challenges and obstacles of the realm of adventure.

The following table draws parallels between the journey of the hero and the veteran.

Stages of the Heroic Journey	**Stages of a Veteran's Experiences Pre- and Post-Deployment**
Hero in Ordinary World	Veteran, Pre-Deployment
Call to Adventure	Orders from Command
Encouragement from Wise Old Man or Woman	Combat Training
Passing the First Threshold to the Adventure Realm	Deployment to the Warzone
Encounters with Helpers, Enemies, Tests and Challenges	Deployment Experiences
Endurance of Supreme Ordeal	Suffering of Traumatic Event
Seizing the Sword	Grasping New Knowledge or Experience
Refusal of the Return	PTSD/Unresolved Traumatic Grief
The Road Back	Natural Recovery

Master of Two Worlds	Post-Traumatic Growth
Freedom to Live	The Ability to Teach/Help Others

Based on this paradigm, post-traumatic stress and unresolved traumatic grief constitute a failure to return. Traumatized veterans have already won the battle, completed the heroic foray into the unknown, but they're still unable to integrate the warrior aspect of themselves into a world that thrives on compassion.

A veteran's goal is to be the "master of two worlds"—that is, to be a wolf and a sheep—having the capacity, when needed, to act in a quick, decisive, perhaps even lethal fashion (as wolf), but tempering this ability with compassion and a belief in the goodness of others (as sheep). This balance is based on real-world experience—not naiveté. Emerging from trauma and post-traumatic stress gives veterans the "freedom to live." This does not necessarily mean that their PTSD-like symptoms will disappear completely or forever, just as the hero's battle scars will remain long after his adventures are over. But the veteran will be able to live his or her life to the fullest and richest extent possible, making quality of life as good or better than it was if the veteran had never experienced a traumatic event.

Hundreds of stories fit this classic structure of the hero's journey: Moses leading the Israelites out of exile, Prometheus stealing fire from the heavens and bringing it to Earth, and Odysseus conquering the Trojans, then battling monsters across the seas for decades before returning home to rule. Veterans lay claim to the same tradition—ordinary human beings who encounter extraordinary circumstances, some that may nearly kill them. Like the heroes of old, veterans have the opportunity to not only survive the challenges of trauma, but grow stronger from the experience, and bestow their boon on themselves and others.

CYCLE OF TRAUMATIC STRESS AND RECOVERY

Combat veterans may assume that once they're out of the military, their risk for trauma drops to nearly nothing. But statistically this isn't true. Combat veterans have more than a 90% chance of experiencing at least one traumatizing event after they've returned from service.[40] The event might be the unexpected or violent death of a loved, one or a serious car accident. The point is this: recovery from trauma, as well as the experience of post-traumatic growth, is not a one-time event. It is a normal, circular process that can occur numerous times over the course of a veteran's life (see figure below). And it is the *capacity to recover from traumatic events, not the ability to avoid them*, that separates those that develop long-term, post-traumatic psychiatric problems from those that go on to lead healthy, productive lives.

The cycle of trauma and recovery occurs through the five stages above. The experience of trauma (Stage 1) triggers biological and psychological symptoms (Stage 2). Veterans then need to regain their basic, innate degree of natural resiliency (Stage 3)—this marks the beginning of the recovery process. Next, a veteran works to finish processing trauma-induced memories and undo trauma-induced

Cycle of Traumatic Stress and Recovery

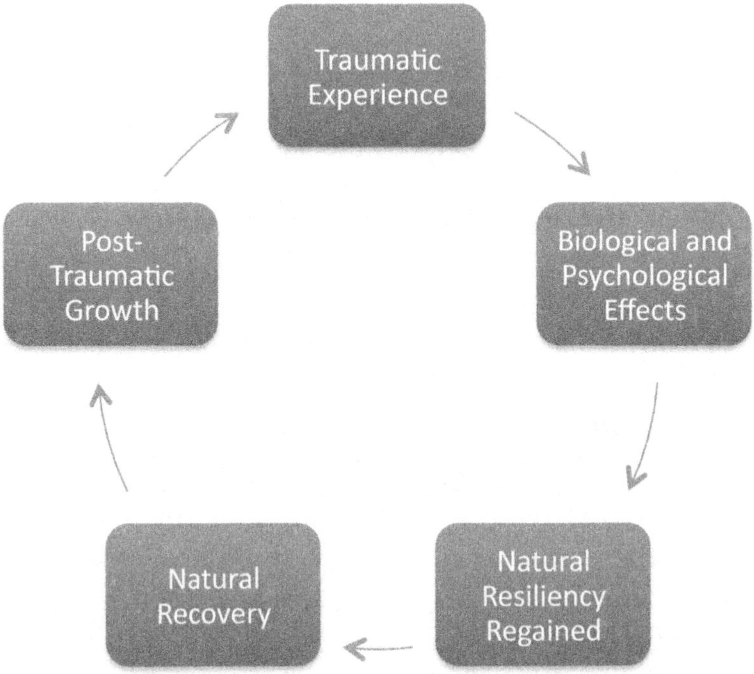

beliefs (stage 4). With time, practice, and the support, veterans can learn to move through these initial four stages relatively quickly, on the order of minutes, hours or days, vs. months, years, decades—or never. Post-traumatic growth (Stage 5) is marked as the final stage of a step-by-step process. In reality, however, things are not so straightforward. Post-traumatic growth and the experience of PTSD are not mutually exclusive. Many, many, veterans experience post-traumatic growth even in the face of ongoing, very disturbing, chronic PTSD-related symptoms.

CHAPTER 18

Increase Veterans' Resiliency

Recovery vs. Resiliency

The concepts of recovery and resiliency are well known in the medical community. They refer to a specific, two-pronged effort to overcome diseases and disorders by preventing the onset of a specific illness (by making people more resilient) or to facilitate recovery from an illness. The traditional resiliency/recovery approach toward the prevention of outbreaks in schools is to (1) make sure that all enrolled children are immunized against specific diseases, and (2) quickly identify and treat any child who becomes sick, so that sickness does not spread.

As we saw earlier, the military has employed various approaches to "inoculate" service members against future deployment-related trauma. The military also encourages veterans to debrief after a traumatic event, as a means to limit the spread of the traumatic "contagion" and minimize the number of service members who develop PTSD or PSTD-type symptoms. The underlying logic is that traumatic experiences, just like any physical illness, are inherently pathological, and best dealt with by minimizing or eliminating the impact on the sufferer. These approaches initially show encouraging results, but the effect is short-lived[41].

It is very difficult, if not impossible, to fully "inoculate" oneself to the experience of trauma. Caring, compassionate people are bound to be biologically and psychologically affected by unexpected, calamitous events. But we can still proactively prepare for such events. Multiple lines of evidence[42] strongly support the claim that specific skills and behaviors can be learned to actively facilitate recovery from trauma. The names for these "skills" and "behaviors" are varied, and there are no commonly agreed-upon terms. In this book, I choose to refer to this capacity to recover as related to ones' degree of "natural resiliency."

INCREASING NATURAL RESILIENCY

Natural resiliency is defined as the innate capacity, in the form of biological and psychological hard-wiring, to recover from unexpected, disturbing, potentially life-threatening experiences. Natural resiliency is akin to a set of tools a person can rely on and utilize to build him or herself back up after a traumatic experience. Someone who tries to write a book without the proper tools—such as a computer, a pencil, a pen and paper—simply won't succeed in his goal because he lacks the means. In the same vein, without the proper biological and psychological tools, no amount of motivation or fortitude by themselves will allow for recovery. Veterans can increase their natural resiliency both before and after exposure to trauma. This is done by increasing the integrity of three aspects of their character: hardiness, compassion, and faith.

HARDINESS

Hardiness is a measure of physical and psychological fortitude, a degree of toughness when it comes to trials in life. Hardiness is vital to the functioning of the limbic brain, which needs to be able to function with enough dedicated energy to finish processing trauma-related memories. If, as a result of injury, a veteran is always in considerable pain or unable to stay focused on one topic or idea, his or her brain may not be up to the task of recovery. By the same token, if a veteran's present life is so stressful and busy that he or she cannot realistically summon the time or emotional energy to deal with past traumatic events, the veteran's brain won't have enough fortitude to fix the problem.

Our brains as well as our bodies need routine exercise to remain in peak condition. Hardiness is achieved through activities and habits—rituals and routines—that increase the functional capacity of the body and brain. Many of these are simple, even obvious. Veterans need to make sure they get enough sleep, eat healthy, exercise regularly, and take time to relax and unwind from the stress of the everyday. Veterans also need to be proactive in addressing undiagnosed or undertreated chronic pain and other medical problems. Intellectual and emotional challenges and problem-solving, as well as striving to maintain deep interpersonal relationships, are crucial to building hardiness.

COMPASSION

You might ask, "Why does a person need to feel compassion for others—not to mention for himself—in order to recover from trauma? Isn't compassion at odds with being tough, being hardy?" While it may not be self-evident, compassion is crucial to developing resiliency. One of the most frequent, and potentially the most devastating, long-term effects of traumatic events is veterans' loss of compassion for themselves. In their own minds, traumatized veterans can feel deep shame or guilt about things that they did—or failed to do—while deployed. As a result, they may feel that they deserve to be punished. When a felon's punishment is handed out by judge or jury, the competing needs of justice have, theoretically, been weighed and balanced. Victims demand harsh justice, but extenuating circumstances, a lack of malicious intent, or genuine repentance on the part of the accused may persuade more lenient punishment. This is the result of mercy, or compassion.

Veterans who feel guilty about past deeds tend to discount the role of compassion and place all their emotional weight on the side of punishment. In effect, they may consciously or unconsciously give themselves a "life sentence" of suffering without parole, and when this happens it becomes extremely difficult, if not impossible, for others to help ease their suffering. In this mental and emotional state of solitary confinement, veterans assume other people "don't know what I did," or that if they were aware, they'd be so repulsed as to agree that the veteran deserves, at the very least, the suffering he's been allotted.

To bounce back from trauma, veterans need to have compassion, and they can cultivate compassion by doing things that better their own lives or the lives of their loved ones. Such activities include simple expressions of gratitude—saying "thank you" in response to some kindness afforded to you from another person. This is a very meaningful, substantial gesture that helps increase our sense of connectedness with other people, and our awareness of their actions on our behalf. Other activities conducive to compassion include making time to help others, being able to forgive oneself and others, and being open to experiencing intense positive emotions like love, joy, and amazement.

Faith

The concept of faith doesn't necessarily depend on a religious belief in a higher power. Faith, in the context of trauma and resiliency, refers to the capacity to believe in things that logic does not compel you to believe in (like trust in other people, as we saw earlier), and hope for things that aren't certain to come about in the future. Many beliefs and hopes are contradicted by facts and evidence that don't support such beliefs at the present time. In 1902, if you were to ask any layman in the nation whether in 30 years they'd be able to board an airplane to fly over the Atlantic, you'd be met with some serious skepticism. But the science of flight developed, and a mastery of aerodynamics changed the world. If in 1960 you asked the average person, regardless of race, ethnicity, or gender, whether the American people would ever elect an African-American president, it would be very hard to find someone with the faith to answer, "Yes." The odds were seen as just too unfavorable, but some believed it was possible, that it would happen, and they fought hard to keep the faith. Ultimately, their beliefs were rewarded.

Veterans with chronic symptoms of post-traumatic stress need to harbor hope that things can get better, even though the harshness of these symptoms and intrusive memories of trauma make a better future seem beyond the realm of possibility. Without faith that things can, against all rational thought and possibility, improve, there's no way anyone can help. A traumatized veteran needs to make this leap on their own so they can be met on the other side by professional therapists, as well as caring friends and family who want to help them improve their lives.

Faith is derived from doing things that explicitly or implicitly have the potential to make our sphere of life more happy, more productive, and more beneficial to ourselves and the people we love. Most veterans already engage in this kind of behavior; they need only acknowledge that fact in order to build their reserves of faith. If a veteran wholeheartedly believed the world was meaningless, only doling out pain and suffering in random, fractured, inconsequential bursts, they wouldn't do things like make long-term plans about where to live or travel, what to study, or what profession to pursue. They wouldn't promote their child's scouting fundraisers or pursuit of a place on the varsity team. They wouldn't feel any reason to go to church or temple. Most tellingly, they wouldn't have borne for so long, be it months, years, or decades, the grief and suffering that has been heaped on them by trauma. In doing any or all of these kinds of things, veterans show that their faith in the world, other people, and themselves has proven resilient to trauma. The goal is to, as the saying goes, "keep on keeping on."

Faith-building activities have a dual benefit. They help veterans deal with trauma-related issues in the short term, and make them more resilient should they encounter trauma in the future.

CHAPTER 19

Encourage Triage-Based Treatment

When it comes to treatment of veterans with, or at risk for, PTSD, there are two schools. One concerns one-on-one treatment for the individual sufferer—the present "sick patient" approach to therapy. The other takes a different tack, reasoning that to help the individual sufferer, we need to inform and empower a population. Since 2001, almost two million service men and women have deployed as part of the Global War on Terror. An estimated 90% will experience at least transient symptoms of post-traumatic stress[43]; 30%, or more than 600,000 veterans, are at risk for developing serious, life-threatening symptoms of PTSD sometime during the course of their lives. An estimated 25% of these veterans will develop "delayed onset" PTSD. This means that while these veterans are currently doing well, without intervention they will develop a threatening psychological condition. But the good news is that there's still time to teach these veterans essential natural recovery skills while these skills are far easier for veterans to learn.

A Different Approach to the Problem of PTSD

The current approach to PTSD from the Department of Veterans Affairs and other government agencies follows the medical model of the "sick" patient. The intent is to encourage veterans suffering with PTSD-like symptoms to first self-identify as being sick and in need of treatment. The treatment follows, in individual or group settings usually lasting eight to twelve weeks.

Psychiatrists and other medical professionals trained in the diagnosis and treatment of PTSD use evidence-based approaches to therapy, with proven results. It's an approach that works, but there are serious limitations. First is the expense—on the order of billions of dollars to treat every veteran with a diagnosis of PTSD.[44] Second, it might not even be possible to find or train enough qualified therapists to take this on given the vast number of veterans diagnosed with PTSD every year.

A fundamentally different approach to treatment views PTSD as a public health concern, one that directly or indirectly impacts us all. Consequently, we all—private citizens, groups, families, and communities—must play key roles in helping mental health professionals heal the "sick." Consider efforts to curtail drunk driving. On the one hand, you have police patrolling the streets, and check points set up to catch offenders before they cause a wreck or kill someone. This is practical, and to some extent effective. But public-awareness campaigns like "friends don't let friends drive drunk," and groups like Mothers Against Drunk Driving (MADD), have a much more pervasive and broad impact on our consciousness. We see these messages and stop to consider, empathize, and find ourselves steering toward responsible choices concerning alcohol and driving before there's a cop in sight to scare us straight.

Triage-Based Care and the Role of Veteran Helpers

If your friend were to fall and injure his ankle, you'd first examine the wound and find out, in your practical opinion, how bad it looks. If your friend's foot is twisted halfway round, if there's bone protruding from the skin, or if your friend is screaming out in pain, you wouldn't hesitate for a second to get to the hospital so that trained medical professionals could respond. But if there's no laceration, if your friend complains of only some mild pain, then the most reasonable course of action may be to ice the ankle, wrap it up, and rest it until it heals. If the ankle becomes worse, you can seek out a doctor; but so long as the symptoms aren't severe and are showing improvement, you've done your friend much good without drawing all kinds of unwanted, unnecessary attention.

Community-based treatment for PTSD follows the same principle. If a veteran's post-deployment problems seem really severe—talk about hurting oneself or committing suicide, or extreme incapacitation that keeps a veteran from performing basic tasks or talking to anyone—don't wait. The problems will only get worse if a trained psychotherapist doesn't get involved. But if the symptoms seem less severe, you can do a lot on your own to pragmatically help a veteran on the road to recovery.

Just as with dependence on alcohol or drugs, it doesn't make sense to intervene only when the damage becomes fully apparent. Veterans, at present, often suffer for months or years with symptoms of PTSD before they get help. The proactive, community-based approach gives all veterans, including those diagnosed with PTSD, an opportunity to learn specific skills to help them naturally recover from trauma. Every veteran's situation is different in terms of the nature and severity of trauma, personal genetics, and other factors that no one can change. Moreover, no degree of training or preparation will fully mitigate all of the suffering and emotional angst associated with unexpected, catastrophic events. But this training can present veterans and veteran helpers with concrete guideposts—referred to as "functional indicators"—to help determine when veterans need additional help.

How to Know if Something's Wrong: Functional Indicators of Post-Trauma Problems

Functional indicators are objective, mutually agreed upon[45] indicators of a veteran's level of functioning at home and at work. They include things such as time spent doing family activities, involvement in hobbies and other recreational activities, professional or academic performance levels, and general life satisfaction. Analogous to the previous discussion about identifying faulty beliefs, the most effective functional indicators are expressed in terms of specific behaviors, not abstractions: telling a veteran he or she seems "distant" may be true, but "distance" is a hard thing to ascertain, identify, or judge, especially if the veteran doesn't see a problem. Pointing out that a veteran has spent the last 12 hours on the computer rather than spending time with family is much more specific and effective in terms of engaging a veteran; these kinds of specific observations also provide a parameter that helps track the progress of improvement.

The first step in helping a veteran who may continue to be affected by deployment-related trauma distress is to identify what, if anything, is wrong. Any major experience is going to change us, and deployment to a combat environment certainly qualifies. The military spends considerable time and energy educating service members and their families on what they can expect, as well as how to prepare for when these soldiers return from overseas. The bottom line is: expect change. When it comes to an individual's personality, however, there's change, and there is *change*. If it's been more than six months or a year since a veteran has been back home, and there still seems to be something very wrong with the way he or she behaves or relates to others, it's time to consider using functional indicators to quantify the degree of this change. Chronic combat-related PTSD, for the most part, does not spontaneously remit—this means that, without intervention, the veteran you are concerned about could potentially have something very wrong with them for the rest of their lives. You don't have to be a clinician or a psychiatrist to help. You don't have to be able to formally diagnose PTSD or any other mental condition. You just have to identify that there's a problem, ascertain what the cause is likely to be, and consider the ways in which you can help. And that's exactly what this book is arming you to do.

Situations often arise where a veteran adamantly denies having any post-trauma problems, including symptoms of PTSD, even though a loved one is convinced that this is not the case. The following describes four categories of functional indicators that veteran helpers can use to determine if a veteran is experiencing chronic, post-deployment PTSD-like problems.

Excessive anxiety strikes at the heart of PTSD. Many trauma-struck veterans are constantly on edge, anxious about threats, and confused by fears that don't seem to have any basis in reality. The symptoms can build to a full-on panic attack, leaving veterans debilitated. What's worse, they don't know why. Anxiety affects sleep, concentration, and relationships with friends and family. Veterans change their behavior and routines to avoid people, places, and things that may trigger intense fears, even when a veteran found these situations comforting in the past.

Excessive irritability and easily getting agitated is a common complaint among veterans with PTSD. They feel that other people are stupid, inconsiderate, and aggravating. Shoppers waste time fumbling in their purses at the checkout. Freeway drivers are too slow or too fast, or too stupid to share the road. The irritable actions of others can snowball into an avalanche of rage for a veteran, which can have disastrous consequences. In extreme cases, veterans report "going red," a dissociative state of rage in which they wreak havoc on people, property, and/or themselves before calming down and coming to. The feeling that everything around them is an irritation is hard for veterans to control or contain. Often veterans take desperate action—reckless driving, self-mutilation, substance abuse—to try to obliterate these intense feelings of rage.

How veterans are perceived by others, after they have been traumatized, is changed in ways both subtle and profound. In ways that is not always easily definable, a returned veteran can seem like they are not same person who went to war. A veteran who used to be easy-going, outgoing, emotionally open or relaxed, might seem serious, terse, aloof, rigid, and emotionally shut off. Loved ones make ultimatums: "Either you get help or the kids and I are leaving." The perception from others that a veteran is going downhill affects the veteran's perception of themselves. They complain of difficulty getting along with other people, whether they're fellow students, workers, or former friends and family. They cease to make or maintain close emotional relationships, because they don't want anyone to get too close. Since these feelings are rooted in how other people see them, veterans feel powerless; they can't change how they're seen by others, and therefore can't change or improve themselves.

Undiagnosed or untreated medical conditions can manifest themselves as unexplained bouts of nausea, vomiting, dizziness, blackouts, or weakness or numbness in their limbs. These medical symptoms often exacerbate other "known" medical problems, such as chronic lower-back pain, seizures, or sleep apnea. The biological toll from both "known" and "unknown" deployment-related medical conditions makes it harder to deal with symptoms of PTSD. This leaves medical professionals in a position of treating veterans with a "snowball effect" of multiple, interrelated, very serious problems, and not always knowing which problem is "causing" the other conditions. This can cause medical professionals to be more tentative in their treatment of these veterans - or worse, put these veterans in a position where medical professionals repeatedly refer treatment until a definitive diagnosis can be made by "someone else." This makes feelings of hopelessness and helplessness even worse, thus increasing the risk for a potentially lethal downward spiral. If it's been more than six months and all of the functional indicators point toward a negative path, don't wait any longer—get the help you need, for yourself, to motivate your loved one to get the help they, in turn, deserve.

CHAPTER 20

Encourage Leaders to Do Their Part

Following the defeat of the Trojans, a victory that relied heavily on his military skill and strategic genius, the ancient Greek hero Odysseus embarked on a post-war journey home to Ithaca. This journey embodied the qualities of strong, self-sacrificial leadership in episode after episode of trials and pitfalls. The powerful sorceress, Circe, imprisons and morphs Odysseus' men; the drunken, lounging Lotus Eaters try to lure Odysseus and his shipmates to their shores; the alluring but deadly Sirens try to take advantage of the wearied sailors' minds and lustful hearts, and Odysseus has himself bound and blindfolded at the mast so as not to be steered off course. In each instance, Odysseus remains steadfast, in words as well as deeds, to his goal of returning each sailor safely home, sound in body and mind. Throughout this mythological adventure home, Odysseus shows his leadership skills are crucial not only amidst the horrors of war, but in its psychological aftermath as well.

The primary aim of this book is to help traumatized veterans lead healthier, more fulfilling lives. **Part I** took on the task of education—helping readers learn about the cause, context, and "cure" for symptoms of post-traumatic stress; this education is an essential precursor for positive change to occur in a veteran's life. **Part II** was concerned with actions—specific, competency-based actions that can help systematically undo the biological and psychological effects of trauma. **Part III** centers on advocacy, driven by individuals, collectives, and leaders, to transform the understanding of PTSD from a pathological, stigma-based issue into something that is a normal part of a veteran's ongoing development—part of a process that is both personal and universal.

Advocacy can take many forms, but first and foremost, advocacy encourages individuals in leadership positions to challenge long-standing assumptions, practices, and rules regarding the prevention, diagnosis, and treatment of PTSD. Leaders, be they corporate, private-sector CEOs, high-ranking politicians, or military officers, are in positions to change the entire context and manner in which we conceptualize PTSD. Leaders operate within strict structural bounds, and even in the best of circumstances, is it never easy for an outsider to convince leaders to change what have been long-held, deploy rooted assumptions. But "if you can imagine it, you can create it." The following section offers an illustration of what this change could look like in a military setting.

Talk in Plain Terms about Trauma

In discussions of trauma and veterans, the term "PTSD" should be taken with a grain of salt. Diagnostic criteria certainly have their place, especially when it comes to implementing effective, evidence-based therapies. But when it comes to helping active-duty service members or veterans define, understand, and come to terms with a specific set of post-traumatic symptoms, calling their condition a "disorder" does little good.

Rather than emphasizing PTSD and its associations with something abnormal or permanently debilitating, leaders can refer to post-traumatic symptoms as a natural and expected consequence of unexpected, horrific events in war that harm veterans themselves, or those they care about. Not every service member will experience trauma, but the reality is that missions can go bad and end with unexpected, unfair, terrible consequences. Tell the troops that if they do experience trauma, post-traumatic symptoms are likely to come up. Explain that the ability to feel compassion—or loyalty, duty, commitment, selfless service, honor—for oneself and others is essential to success in combat, enabling service members to act heroically, sustain long periods of deprivation and suffering, all while remaining motivated to fight through extended trials. No matter what terminology is used to describe it, compassion is crucial to the military's long-term success.

As we've seen, the capacity to care must be present for a veteran to be traumatized, and *leaders need to make that fact very plain*—some of the qualities that make someone a good soldier also makes him or her more likely to develop post-traumatic symptoms. There are ways to assuage the intensity of post-traumatic stress through preventative measures, but a service member's deployment and capacity to care makes him or her vulnerable to post-traumatic stress. There's no sense trying to hide or dance around this reality—it does no service to veterans, their families, or the efficient, elite functioning of the military itself.

Chart a Realistic Course Toward Recovery

Earlier, we reviewed the concept of post-traumatic growth, which demonstrates how, in the long run, traumatized veterans can function at a higher, more effective level—in their personal as well as professional and/or military lives—than they did prior to their exposure to trauma. This is a highlight of recovery that veterans need to be aware of, and there are other truths about the recovery process that dispel misconceptions of what it means to "get better" following a traumatic experience.

Leaders should strive to emphasize and help implement experience-based competencies and skill-development such as that outlined in the GROWTH method. Veterans may be distraught as a result of trauma, feeling both hopeless and helpless, doomed to a life plagued by harsh symptoms stemming from trauma. Leaders' emphasis on a step-by-step course of gradual recovery speaks in an impassioned, direct, and personal way to these veterans, who will respond better to such an approach than to one that is strictly objective, "scientific," "logical," or impersonal. Remember to emphasize that no recovery method will make symptoms disappear entirely. But through such methods, and supported by professional therapy (when needed), traumatized veterans can make the intensity of these symptoms die down, allowing them to lead the lives they choose rather than lives governed by traumatic stress.

Institute Educational Courses Concerning Post-Traumatic Stress

Each branch of the U.S. military requires its service members to attend certain pre-deployment and post-deployment classes or seminars. These courses deal with traditional outcomes or fallout from having been in the service; trouble in a marriage and financial problems are two of the most pervasive subjects.

In addition to the current roster, military leaders should consider adding competency-based education about post-traumatic stress to the agenda. This kind of course helps service members gain the specific skills necessary to undo trauma-related faulty beliefs and finish processing trauma-induced, partially processed memories. Unlike the other skills currently taught, the solutions to post-traumatic, stress-related problems are not intuitive, obvious, or self-evident. As we've noted many times throughout this book, logic can actually create roadblocks to recovery; we need to institute specific courses that teach veterans skills they can use to combat the onset and symptoms of post-traumatic stress. Evidence shows that the intensity of post-traumatic stress can be reduced so that a given veteran can live a life unfettered by his or her symptoms. The fact that up to 15% of traumatized veterans still seriously consider or attempt suicide as a means to alleviate their suffering is an inexcusable statistic that leaders need to work to draw down through preventative educational courses that explain to veterans what the condition means, and how they can rise above it.

In the end, leaders can help veterans through large-scale, structural changes as to how we learn about and talk about post-traumatic stress. Veteran helpers can give veterans the encouragement they need to take their recovery along a new, effective path of experience. Veterans help themselves by staying open to the possibility of hope, happiness, closeness with others, and care for themselves—even when such spirits defy all logic. Use the knowledge and methods you've learned from this book to create change in the system and in yourself, and never be ashamed to seek the help you need from a professional, a leader, or a loved one.

APPENDIX A

Presentation of PTSD in Combat Veterans

Books:

Tears of a Warrior: A family's story of combat and living with PTSD, Janet J. Sheahorn, PhD, E. Anthony Sheahorn, MBA, 2008

A personal account from a Vietnam combat veteran and his wife on how PTSD effected their lives, as well as what they did to overcome these problems.

Faces of Combat PTSD and TBI (one journalist's crusade to improve treatment for our veterans) Eric Newhouse, 2008

Written from numerous interviews with veterans, Mr. Newhouse tells the story of the struggles and challenges many veterans face upon their return to civilian life after deployments to Iraq and Afghanistan.

Down Range: to Iraq and Back; Bridget C. Cantrell, PhD, and Chuck Dean, 2005

Based on first-hand accounts of Iraqi veterans, this book gives voice to the challenges faced by many returning combat veterans, as well as practical advice on what to do to meet these challenges.

Online Information:

Real Warriors, Real Battles, Real Strength
www.Realwarriors.net
Sponsored by the Defense Centers for Excellence, this website offers an excellent array of personal stories from returning combat veterans on the serious, and even life threatening challenges they faced prior to getting the help they needed.

Make the Connection
www.Maketheconnection.net
Sponsored by the Department of Veteran Affairs, this site allows veterans to hear inspiring stories of strength and resolve to overcome PTSD, thoughts of suicide, and related problems.

National Center for PTSD
www.ncptsd.org

Sponsored by the Department of Veteran Affairs, a very informative website on the signs and symptoms of PTSD, as well as co-occurring problems.

APPENDIX B

References

BOOKS:

Alverez, A. (1970). *The Savage God: A Study of Suicide.* New York: Random House.

Campbell, J. (1972). *The Hero with a Thousand Faces.* New Jersey: Princeton University Press; 2nd edition

Herman, J. (1992, 1997). *Trauma and Recovery: The Aftermath of Violence—from Domestic Abuse to Political Terror*, New York: Basic Books.

Meichenbaum, *D. A. (2003). Clinical Handbook/Practical Therapist Manual for Assessing and Treating Adults with Post-Traumatic Stress Disorder (PTSD).* Chicago. Institute Press

Litz, B.T. (editor) (2004) *Early Intervention for Trauma and Traumatic Loss.* New York: The Guilford Press.

Najavits LM (2006). *Seeking Safety A Treatment Manual for PTSD and Substance Abuse.* New York: The Guilford Press.

Jacobs, S. (1999) *Traumatic Grief: Diagnosis, Treatment, and Prevention* (The Series in Trauma and Loss), New York: Taylor and Francis

Walsh, F. (2006), *Strengthening Family Resilience*, Second Edition (Guilford Family Therapy Series). New York: The Guilford Press.

Yehuda, Rachel, McFarlane, Alexander C. (editors) *(1997) Psychobiology of Posttraumatic Stress Disorder: A decade of progress.* New York: Annals of the New York Academy of Sciences, Volume 821

ARTICLES:

Best, S.R., Lipsey T.L., &Weiss D.S. (2003) *Predictors of posttraumatic stress disorder and symptoms in adults: a meta-analysis. Psychol Bull*, 129(1), 52-73

Bisson, J.,& Andrew, M. (2007) *Psychological treatment of post-traumatic stress disorder (PTSD).Cochrane Database Syst Rev*, 18(3), CD003388.

Bisson J.I., et al. (2007) *Psychological treatments for chronic post-traumatic stress disorder: systematic review and meta-analysis. Br J Psychiatry*, 190, 97-104.

Bormann, J.E., Thorp S., Wetherell, J.L., & Golshan, S.A., (2008) *Spiritually based group intervention for combat veterans with posttraumatic stress disorder: feasibility study. J Holist Nurs*, 26(2), 109-16..

Bradley D., et al, (2004) *A National Longitudinal Study of the Psychological Consequences of the September 11,*

Terrorist Attacks: Reactions, Impairment and Help-Seeking, Psychiatry, 67(2) 105-117

Breslau N., Kessler R.C., Chilcoat, H.D, Schultz LR, Davis G.C., & Andreski, P. (1998) *Trauma and posttraumatic stress disorder in the community: the 1996 Detroit Area Survey of Trauma. Arch Gen Psychiatry,* 1998 55(7),626-32.

Brewin C.R., Andrews B, &Valentine J.D.(2000) *Meta-analysis of risk factors for posttraumatic stress disorder in trauma-exposed adults. J Consult Clin Psychol,* 68(5),748-66.

Brewin CR, & Holmes EA.(2003) *Psychological theories of posttraumatic stress disorder. Clin Psychol Rev,* 2003 May; 23(3):339-76

Briere, J. *Dissociative symptoms and trauma exposure: specificity, affect dysregulation, and Posttraumatic stress,* J Nerv Ment Dis. 2006 Feb;194(2):78-82

Cameron R, & Meichenbaum D. *Cognition and behavior change, Aust N Z J Psychiatry,* 1980 Jun;14(2):121-5.

Cole J. *Painful memories: ritual and the transformation of community trauma. Cult Med Psychiatry,* 2004 Mar;28(1):87-105

Cottraux J, Note, I, Yao SN, de Mey-Guillard C, Bonasse F, Djamoussian D, Mollard E, Note B, & Chen Y. *Randomized controlled comparison of cognitive behavior therapy with Rogerian supportive therapy in chronic post-traumatic stress disorder: a 2-year follow-up. Psychother Psychosom,* 2008;77(2):101-10. Epub 2008 Jan 25.

Everly G.S, & Mitchell, J.T. (2000) *The debriefing "controversy" and crisis intervention: a review of lexical and substantive issues. Int J Emerg Ment Health*, 2(4):211-25.

Fairbank, J.A., Hough R.L., Jordan B.K., Marmar C.R, & Weiss, D.S. *The psychological risks of Vietnam: the NVVRS perspective*, J Trauma Stress. 2007 Aug;20(4):467-79

Foa, E.B. 2006 *Psychosocial therapy for posttraumatic stress disorder. J Clin Psychiatry*; 67 Suppl 2:40-5.

Foa EB, & Meadows, E.A. (1997)*Psychosocial treatments for posttraumatic stress disorder: a critical review. Annu Rev Psychol*,48:449-80.

Friedman MJ, &Pitman RK. (2007) *New findings on the neurobiology of posttraumatic stress disorder. J Trauma Stress*, 20(5),653-5.

Heinrichs M, Wagner D, Schoch W, Soravia LM, Hellhammer DH, & Ehlert U. (2005) *Predicting posttraumatic stress symptoms from pretraumatic risk factors: a 2-year prospective follow-up study in firefighters. Am J Psychiatry*,162(12), 2276-86.

Landau J, Mittal M, & Wieling E. (2008) *Linking human systems: strengthening individuals, families, and communities in the wake of mass trauma. J Marital Fam Ther*, 34(2), 193-209

Lapierre CB, Schwegler AF, & Labauve BJ. (2007) *Posttraumatic stress and depression symptoms in soldiers returning from combat operations in Iraq and Afghanistan. J Trauma Stress*, 20(6),933-43.

Leszcz M, Yalom ID, & Norden M (1995)*The value of inpatient group psychotherapy: patients' perceptions. Int J Group Psychother,* 35(3), 411-33.

Malta LS, Wyka KE, Giosan C, Jayasinghe N, & Difede J. (2009) *Numbing symptoms as predictors of unremitting posttraumatic stress disorder. J Anxiety Disord,* 23(2), 223-9

Nemeroff CB, Bremner JD, Foa EB, Mayberg HS, North CS, & Stein MB. (2006) *Posttraumatic stress disorder: a state-of-the-science J Psychiatr Res,*40(1),1-21.

Ozer EJ, Oflaz F, Hatipo lu S, & Aydin H. (2008) *Effectiveness of psychoeducation intervention on post-traumatic stress disorder and coping styles of earthquake survivors. J Clin Nurs,* 17(5),677-87.

Ozer EJ, Best SR, Lipsey TL, &Weiss DS. (2003) *Predictors of posttraumatic stress disorder and symptoms in adults: a meta-analysis. Psychol Bull,*129(1), 52-73.

Pennebaker JW. (1993) *Putting stress into words: health, linguistic, and therapeutic implications. Behav Res Ther,*31(6),539-48.

Berry DS, & Pennebaker JW. (1993) *Nonverbal and verbal emotional expression and health. Psychother Psychosom,*59(1),11-9.

Peterson C, Park N, Pole N, D'Andrea W, &Seligman ME. (2008) *Strength of character and posttraumatic growth J Trauma Stress,* 2008 21(2),214-7.

Richards JM, Beal WE, Seagal JD, &Pennebaker JW. (2000) *Effects of disclosure of traumatic events on illness behavior among psychiatric prison inmates. J Abnorm Psychol,*109(1),156-60.

Rothbaum BO, Davis M. (2003) *Applying learning principles to the treatment of post-trauma reactions. Ann N Y Acad Sci,*1008,112-21.

Rundell JR, Ursano RJ, Holloway HC, & Silberman EK. (1989) *Psychiatric responses to trauma. Hosp Community Psychiatry,*40(1),68-74.

Schlenger WE, Kulka RA, Lating JM, &Bono SF. *Crisis intervention and fostering resiliency.(2008) Int J Emerg Ment Health,*10(2):87-93

Schlenger WE, Kulka RA, Fairbank JA, Hough RL, Jordan BK, Marmar CR, &Weiss DS. (2007) *The psychological risks of Vietnam: the NVVRS perspective. J Trauma Stress,* 20(4),467-79.

Tedeschi, R,G., Calhoun, L.G. (1996) *The Post-Traumatic Growth Inventory: Measuring the Positive Legacy of Trauma,* J. Trauma Stress, 9(3):455-71

van der Kolk BA, & Fisler RE. (1994) *Childhood abuse and neglect and loss of self-regulation. Bull Menninger Clin,*58(2),145-68.

End Notes

[1] The military uses the hands on a clock to denote location. "Six" refers to an area behind you.

[2] According to the criteria presented in the *Diagnostic and Statistical Manual-IV-TR*; the official diagnostic nomenclature used by mental health professionals

[3] To differentiate between the different meanings of "post-traumatic", the followings terms are used in this book: "post-traumatic stress" describes potentially transient, post-trauma symptoms; "PTSD" describes individuals who have been formally diagnosed with PTSD; and "PTSD-like" describes individuals have chronic (more than six month) severe, post-trauma impairment, but who have not been diagnosed by a professional as having a specific psychiatric condition.

[4] negative re-enforcement is the technical term for 'punishment'

[5] SGT Audie Murphy is the quintessential example of a compassionate killer. He was an exceptional marksman and tactician. Over the course of World War II, he is credited with killing 240 enemy combatants. In one battle, for which he received the Medal of Honor, he single handedly fought against 250 Germans and six tanks, killing or wounding 50 of them. When asked, later in life, why he did this seemly impossible task, he answered simply "they were killing my friends." The Audie Murphy Club is a privately run, extremely prestigious organization whose membership is only made available to NCO's who display 'outstanding capacity for helping fellow soldiers and their families'.

[6] Marshall, SLA, *Men Against Fire: The Problem of Battle Command*, Washington: Infantry Journal, New York, William Morrow & Co. c1947

[7] Turner, MA, et al, *Acute military psychiatric casualties from the war in Iraq. Br J Psychiatry*, 2005, Jun; 186: 476-9. This is in compari-

son to the almost 400,000 "combat stress casualties" needing evacuation during WWII.

[8] In the 1970s, psychoanalysis and psychoanalytical thought formed the basis for most DSM-related decisions. This meant that the individual's internal psychological state, and not his or her external circumstances, were deemed to be the most important determinate in who developed psychopathology. The creation of the DSM-III, in 1980, was a landmark achievement in that it represented a fundamental shift from "individual centered" pathology to "statistically based," or "empirically based" pathology - a shift that resulted, as we will discuss, in some advantages as well as unintended adverse consequences.

[9] Swank, R.L., Marchand, W.E., (1946) *Combat Neurosis: Development of Combat Exhaustion, Arch.* Nuer Psych 55: 236-247

[10] Breslau N, Davis GC. (1987) Posttraumatic stress disorder: the etiologic specificity of wartime stressors. Am J Psychiatry. May;144(5):578-83.

[11] Reprinted from public assess website: http://www.mccscp.com/combat-operational-stress

[12] Hoge CW, McGurk D, Thomas JL, Cox AL, Engel CC, Castro CA. (2008) *Mild traumatic brain injury in U.S. soldiers returning from Iraq.* N Engl J Med. 358(5):453-63 - Dr. Hoge also demonstrated that even in veterans with a Traumatic Brain Injury (TBI) - PTSD causes a significant number of somatic, TbI-like symptoms - Hoge C.W, et al, (2007) *Association of posttraumatic stress disorder with somatic symptoms, health care visits, and absenteeism among Iraq war veterans.* Am J Psychiatry. 164(1):150–153

[13] This is an over generalization *–for example, an explosion or blast directly in front of service* member will cause more damage to the frontal lobes and a blast that occurs from the either side will general cause more damage to the temporal lobes.

[14] This is true in chronic, long-term effects of traumatic brain injuries; acute injuries cause unique cellular effects. In addition, blast injuries also cause diffuse axonal Injury (DAI). For more information on the effects of blast injuries, I recommend the Department of Defense and Veterans Affairs brain injury's website: www.dvbic.org

[15] Interestingly enough, treatment with antidepressants, such as Zoloft, which treat PTSD, are known to promote neurogenesis in the dendrite nucleus - for a review please see Malberg, J.E. et al. (2000) *Chronic antidepressant treatment increases neurogenesis in adult rat hippocampus.* J. Neurosci. 20: 9104–9110

[16] Dr. Shneidman discusses his concept of psychache at length in his book *Suicide as Psychache* (1993) Rowman & Littlefield Publishers, Lanham, Maryland

[17] Dr. Uvanas - Moberg is among a group of researchers studying this phenomenon. For a review, please see - Uvanas - Moberg, K., (1996) *Neuroendocrinology of the mother-child interaction,* Trends Endocrinol Metab. 7(4) 126-31

[18] Spitz, R.A. (1946) Anaclitic depression: an inquiry into the genesis of psychiatric conditions in early childhood, Psychoanal Study Child; 2313 - 42

[19] Blaustein, M, Fleming A., (2009) *Suicide from the Golden Gate Bridge*, Am J Psychiatry. 166(10): 111-6

[20] For more information about Dr. Joiner's theory of suicide, please refer to his book *Why People Commit Suicide*, (2005), Harvard University Press, 2005

[21] This rate is a low estimate, given the life-time prevalence of suicidal ideation of about 14% for the general population. (reference: Kessler R.C., Borges G., Walters E.E., (1999) *Prevalence of and risk factors for lifetime suicide attempts in the National Comorbidity Survey.* Arch Gen Psychiatry. 56(7):617-26.) Combat Veterans have a high rate of additional factors known to increase suicide risk such as depression, substance abuse, traumatic brain injury and PTSD.

[22] The study concludes that since there is not a statistical increase in the number of suicides among deployed service members, deployment related trauma must not be a factor. The report fails to mention that suicide may be a delayed response to trauma exposure, as it has been in the case of innumerable Vietnam veterans. Traumatized veterans may self-select to leave the service, so that true number of deployment related suicides is grossly under-estimated by only tracking active duty personnel who consider and or complete suicide

[23] It is called "natural" debriefing, because the process occurs naturally and without a need for any prior instruction or education.

[24] Dr. Victor Frankel, psychiatrist, creator of logotherapy, and a survivor of a concentration camp during WWII, postulated that one can endure incredible suffering as long as one finds meaning in it - for more information about Dr. Frankel, I recommend his seminal work *Man's Search for Meaning, (1946),* Beacon Press, Boston, MA

[25] The technical term to describe this change is "allosteric dysregulation." The body normally maintains a "homeostatic" equilibrium - that is to say, the body attempts to keep things, like the amount of sodium in our blood, the same in the face of external stressors that attempt to disrupt this equilibrium. "Allosteric" refers to the pro-

cessing of actively creating disequilibrium in response to a specific stress. The "fight or flight" response is an example of allosteric regulation, because the body activity does several things, such as increase the heart rate and blood pressure that actively moves the body away from a homeostatic state.

[26] Biologically speaking, veterans with PTSD are different than veterans without PTSD in that (1) they have an abnormally low threshold for response to perceived threat; (2) they are hyper-responsive to perceived threat - they productive excessive amounts of cortisol and other stress related hormones; and (3) they do not habituate once the perceived threat is over - that is to say, they are biologically "hard wired" to have a very difficult time calming down once a perceived threat has ended.

[27] I discuss several relaxation techniques in the Traumatic Stress Recovery for Veteran's Workbook, available through www.resiliencyservices.com. Additional resources to help veterans practice specific relaxation techniques are www.afterdeployment.org and www.Hooahforhealth.org

[28] Eye Movement Desensitization and Reprocessing (EMDR) exploit this principle, and is one of the reasons for the efficacy of this technique. Of note: the efficacy and limits of efficacy of EMDR is a very controversial topic among researchers and clinicians.

[29] Cognitive Behavioral Therapy is based upon the premise that one can dramatically decrease the intensity of PTSD symptoms by addressing, dysfunctional trauma-induced thoughts. In practice, CPT therapy can nicely compliment the ideas and suggestions made in this book. For a review of the efficacy of CPT, see Marks I et al, (1998) *Treatment of posttraumatic stress disorder by exposure and/or cognitive restructuring: a controlled study.* Arch Gen Psychiatry. Apr;55(4):317-25

[30] For additional help in identifying ways to help veterans identify as well as effectively deal with unresolved traumatic grief, I recommend my companion book, *Traumatic Stress Recovery for Veterans.* I also recommend Jennifer Wilkerson's book, *The Essence of Being Real: Relational Peer Support for Men and Women Who Have Experienced Trauma,* (2002) Sidran Press.

[31] In addition to talking about prior trauma, writing down and reading (and re-reading) stories of traumatic events is also an effect way to help the brain process trauma-induced, limbic memories. For more information about the effectiveness of writing about prior trauma, please see Pennebaker J.W., Beall S.K., (1986) *Confronting a traumatic*

event: toward an understanding of inhibition and disease. J Abnorm Psychol. 95(3):274-81

[32] From a scientific perspective, the capacity to self-regulate is related to the parasympathetic (break) system. The effect of trauma is to create a situation where veteran's fight or flight response is so powerful and sustained that it exceeds that veteran's capacity to self-sooth/calm down. Biologically speaking, veteran helpers act like an external "parasympathetic system" that increases the capacity of veterans' parasympathetic system to "calm down", even in what were previously intolerable, trauma-related feelings. For an extensive review of the association between biology and the capacity to self-sooth, see Dr. Alan Shore's book, (1999) *Affect regulation and the origin of the self: The Neurobiology of Emotional Development, Lawrence Erlbaum Assoc., Inc.*

[33] As discussed by Dr. Katz in his book, *On Playing a Poor Hand Well: Insights from the Lives of Those Who Have Overcome Childhood Risks and Adversities* (1997), Norton Professional Books, the person who provides this 'holding environment' for a growing child need not be a biological parent; any individual, be it a grandparent, foster parent, or a consistent member in that child's community can fulfill this role.

[34] For example, this is true in long-term, follow up of individuals in New York City after the September 11, 2001 terrorist attacks (Reference: Neria, Y., et al, (2010) *Long-term course of probable PTSD after the 9/11 attacks: a study in urban primary care.* J Trauma Stress. 23(4):474-82)

[35] For a review of the efficacy of evidence based treatment of PTSD, please see Bisson, J.I., et al. (2007) *Psychological treatments for chronic post-traumatic stress disorder: systematic review and meta-analysis. Br J Psychiatry*, 190, 97-104.

[36] In a manner similar to the logic by which I call debriefing "natural," I refer to recovery as a "natural" process that is innate, natural, and not something learned through formal education.

[37] Tedeschi, R,G., Calhoun, L.G. (1996) *The Post-Traumatic Growth Inventory: Measuring the Positive Legacy of Trauma*, J. Trauma Stress, 9(3):455-71

[38] Ibid - p.455

[39] Campbell, J. (1972). *The Hero with a Thousand Faces.* New Jersey: Princeton University Press; 2nd edition p. 30

[40] Part of the reason for this is prior exposure to trauma, for a number of reasons, greatly increases one's risk for future exposure to poten-

tially traumatizing events. For a review please see Orcutt, H.K., Erikson, D.J., Wolfe, J., (2002) *A prospective analysis of trauma exposure: the mediating role of PTSD symptomatology.* J. Traumatic Stress 15(3): 259-266

41 "Critical incident debriefings," which are structured debriefings meant to help veterans process the experience of a traumatic event and decrease associated long-term problems, are no longer used. This is because several meta-analyses revealed that traumatized individuals who underwent critical incident debriefings had an equal or higher long-term risk for developing PTSD than those who did not undergo these debriefings. This is still a controversial issue.

42 Over the past 40 years, more than 50 variables have been identified that affect one's capacity to recover from post-traumatic stress and post-traumatic stress disorder symptoms. For a review, see Meichenbaum, D.A. (2004) *Clinical Handbook/Practical Therapist Manual for Assessing and Treating Adults with Post-Traumatic Stress Disorder (PTSD). Chicago.* Institute Press

43 One of the reasons the "time" criteria was added to the DSM-III Diagnosis of PTSD is that symptoms of PTSD lasting less than four weeks often spontaneously remit on their own. As noted above, in single incidence of traumatic experiences, one must wait at least a month before these symptoms are "chronic" - i.e. do not go away on their own.

44 According to a report released by the Congressional Budget Office (2012), a cost of treating veterans with PTSD with or without a co-occurring traumatic brain injury is about $10,000 per veteran (reference: http://www.cbo.gov/sites/default/files/cbofiles/attachments/02-09-PTSD.pdf) Assuming an average length of treatment of one year, the total cost of treating the estimated 500-800,000 WGOT veterans who will get PTSD treatment would be between five to eight trillion dollars. Of note: For many veterans, treatment is indefinite. So in actual practice, the total cost of treatment would be much greater.

45 It is not uncommon for spouses to feel that there is a serious problem while their veteran husband or wife denies or minimizes the significance of this problem. In this case, it is important to emphasize that in a relationship, what is seen as a problem for one partner is, by definition, *also* a problem and a concern for the other. Hence, if a spouse is concerned about a veteran's behavior, then it is the veteran's responsibility to address this concern out of respect for his or her spouse.

About the Author:

David A. Fohrman, M.D. is a board-certified child, adolescent, and adult psychiatrist. He is the founder of Traumatic Stress Recovery with more than 12 years of experience teaching resiliency techniques in both military and civilian settings. While serving as Chief of Mental Health in the 1st Armored Division, Dr. Fohrman created a stress resiliency program. The program was so successful that many of its elements have subsequently become the Army-wide standard of care for increasing the resiliency of forward deployed soldiers. Dr. Fohrman is the recipient of numerous awards, including Alpha Omega Alpha, the Kosovo Campaign Ribbon, and America's Top Psychiatrists (2006). From 2008 to 2012, while working in the VA system, Dr. Fohrman was able to use his Traumatic Stress Recovery program to dramatically improve the quality of life for over 900 veterans, family members, and members of the national air and army guard. He is the co-founder of resiliency services and works to provide education, prevention, and treatment for individual's traumatized as a result of work-related selfless service.

CPSIA information can be obtained
at www.ICGtesting.com
Printed in the USA
BVOW06s1416071216
470048BV00009B/232/P

9 781457 517785